CANYON CAFE
SAM'S CAFE & DESERT FIRE

BRINGING THE SOUTHWEST EXPERIENCE HOME

DESIGNED, WRITTEN & PRODUCED BY:
THE EXLINE AGENCY
939 BROADWAY
DENVER, CO 80203
303-893-4343

CREATIVE VISION & EXECUTIVE MANAGEMENT: MIKE LIEDBERG & DOUG CZUFIN, CANYON CAFE

PHOTOGRAPHY: RICK SOUDERS & TREVOR MOORE, SOUDERS STUDIOS, GOLDEN, CO
ILLUSTRATIONS: MEGAN MORGAN, STRANGE BIRD DESIGNS, STEAMBOAT SPRINGS, CO
ART DIRECTION & PROJECT MANAGEMENT: LISA KRUEGER & AMY HAMILTON, THE EXLINE AGENCY

PRINTED & BOUND IN THE USA BY KEYLINE GRAPHICS, DENVER, CO

SPECIAL THANKS TO JACK AND ROBIN OF THE NATIVE AMERICAN TRADING COMPANY,
DENVER, FOR THE KIND LOAN OF MANY UNIQUE AND BEAUTIFUL ARTIFACTS.

Table of Contents

Dear Friends,

After many requests and long preparation, we have compiled some favorite recipes that celebrate the people, cultures and cuisine of the American Southwest. The chefs from our three sister restaurants: Canyon Cafe, Sam's Cafe and Desert Fire share a love for this cuisine because of the endless variety it offers.

A region of deserts, farmlands, mountains, canyons, plains and vineyards; the Southwest inspires a special way of life—one where time is measured by the changing of the seasons, rather than the ticking of the clock.

We created this cookbook to reflect this appealing way of life. It is divided into seasonal sections with four "experience" menus in each, to help you bring the Southwest home, wherever you happen to live. As you read, look for this symbol ⌣ which indicates ingredients defined in callouts throughtout the book and in the glossary.

We hope you come to love the Southwest experience as much as we do. We look forward to welcoming you to our restaurants soon.

First Day of Spring
The Birds & The Bees
Just Among Friends
Three Sisters

Spring

Chile Shrimp Kabobs with
Papaya-Mango Salsa

Fiesta Slaw

Cilantro Pesto Rice

Apple-Piñon Empanadas

Red Rock Lemonade

First Day of Spring

There is a day every year when you suddenly realize Spring
has finally arrived. We created this menu to celebrate that
day with flavorful, refreshing dishes designed to set the
stage for the wonders of the season.

Our *Chile Shrimp Kabobs* are long-time favorites from
the grill. Serve the kabobs on a colorful bed of *Fiesta Slaw*
accompanied by tasty *Cilantro Pesto Rice.* Garnish the plate
with the fresh *Papaya-Mango Salsa* to create a delightful
palette that will be pleasing to the senses. Complete this
meal with *Apple-Piñon Empanadas* for dessert and our
signature *Red Rock Lemonade.*

CHILE SHRIMP KABOBS WITH PAPAYA-MANGO SALSA

SERVES: 6

Directions:

Lemon Butter

1. HEAT JUICE IN A 2 QT. SAUCE PAN OVER MEDIUM HEAT.

2. BEGIN WHISKING IN CUBES OF BUTTER ONE AT A TIME UNTIL EMULSIFIED (CREAMY LOOKING). DO THIS OVER LOW HEAT TO PREVENT THE SAUCE FROM SEPARATING.

3. SEASON WITH SALT AND PEPPER IF DESIRED. KEEP IN A WARM AREA, BUT NOT ON DIRECT HEAT.

Kabobs

1. BEFORE USING, SOAK THE SKEWERS IN HOT WATER FOR ABOUT AN HOUR (SO THEY DON'T BURN WHEN ON THE GRILL).

2. MIX SOY SAUCE AND OLIVE OIL TOGETHER WITH MUSTANG SPICE™.

3. THREAD ALL VEGETABLES AND SHRIMP ON SKEWERS IN THE FOLLOWING ORDER: MUSHROOM, SHRIMP, ONION, TOMATO, GREEN PEPPER, ONION, SHRIMP, ONION, RED PEPPER, SHRIMP AND MUSHROOM.

4. BRUSH ON MARINADE AND PLACE ON A HOT GRILL.

5. COOK EACH SIDE OF KABOB APPROXIMATELY 3 MINUTES OR UNTIL SHRIMP TURN PINK.

6. SERVE OVER CILANTRO RICE (PAGE 11). TOP EACH KABOB WITH PAPAYA-MANGO SALSA (PAGE 81) AND DRIZZLE WITH LEMON BUTTER. GREAT SERVED WITH HOT BUTTERED CORN ON THE COB.

* See page 87 for Mustang Spice™ recipe.

Ingredients:

Lemon Butter

4 OZ. LEMON JUICE (ABOUT 4 LEMONS, JUICED)

1 LB. UNSALTED BUTTER, CUBED

SALT & PEPPER TO TASTE

Kabobs

12 (10") WOODEN SKEWERS, SOAKED IN HOT WATER FOR ABOUT AN HOUR

6 TBSP. SOY SAUCE

4 TBSP. OLIVE OIL

2 TBSP. MUSTANG SPICE™*

24 MEDIUM MUSHROOMS, CLEANED

36 JUMBO SHRIMP, PEELED & DE-VEINED, WITH TAILS LEFT ON

2 WHITE ONIONS, CUT INTO 1" SQUARES

6 ROMA TOMATOES, CUT IN HALF

3 GREEN PEPPERS, CUT INTO 1" SQUARES

3 RED PEPPERS, CUT INTO 1" SQUARES

1 RECIPE PAPAYA-MANGO SALSA

SERVES: 6

FIESTA SLAW

Ingredients:

Dressing

1 RECIPE CHILE-LIME
    VINAIGRETTE*

3 TBSP. SESAME OIL

1/2 CUP SUGAR

Slaw

1 HEAD RED OR GREEN
    CABBAGE, SHREDDED
    (RINSED IF RED)

2 RED BELL PEPPERS,
    JULIENNED

2 YELLOW BELL PEPPERS,
    JULIENNED

3 CARROTS, PEELED &
    JULIENNED

3 ZUCCHINI, JULIENNED
    (GREEN PARTS ONLY)

1 LARGE RED ONION,
    RINSED & JULIENNED

3 YELLOW SQUASH,
    JULIENNED (YELLOW
    PARTS ONLY)

Directions:

1. TO MAKE THE DRESSING, MIX CHILE-LIME VINAIGRETTE
    (PAGE 46), SESAME OIL AND SUGAR IN A LARGE BOWL.
    WHISK UNTIL SUGAR IS DISSOLVED.

2. TOSS IN REMAINING INGREDIENTS AND CHILL 30 MINUTES
    BEFORE SERVING.

* See page 46 for Chile-Lime Vinaigrette recipe.

CILANTRO PESTO RICE

SERVES: 6

Directions:

1. Place cilantro, pine nuts, parmesan and garlic in a food processor. Begin processing at high speed, then add lime juice. Drizzle in oil to make a smooth paste. Season with salt and pepper.

2. Heat stock in a shallow sauce pan. Add rice and stir.

3. Cover and let simmer for about 15 minutes or until most of the liquid is absorbed.

4. Add 1 cup of the pesto and cover. Cook 5 more minutes. Turn off heat and let rest 5 more minutes.

5. Gently stir pico de gallo into rice. (This gives some contrasting color, freshness and an extra bit of flavor.)

6. Serve hot.

* See page 49 for Pico de Gallo recipe.

Ingredients:

Pesto

2 BUNCHES CILANTRO, WASHED & STEMMED

1/3 CUP PINE NUTS, LIGHTLY TOASTED

1/4 CUP PARMESAN CHEESE, SHREDDED

1 TBSP. FRESH GARLIC, MINCED

1 TBSP. FRESH-SQUEEZED LIME JUICE

1/4 CUP EXTRA VIRGIN OLIVE OIL

1 TSP. SALT

1/2 TSP. FRESH-GROUND BLACK PEPPER (OR TO TASTE)

Rice

3 CUPS CONVERTED LONG GRAIN RICE

5 CUPS CHICKEN OR VEGETABLE STOCK

1/2 TSP. SALT

1 CUP PICO DE GALLO*

SERVES: 6

APPLE-PIÑON EMPANADAS

Ingredients:

1 RECIPE DOUBLE
CRUST PASTRY

Filling

2 LARGE GRANNY
SMITH APPLES

1 TBSP. LIME JUICE

4 TBSP. BUTTER

1/4 CUP GOLDEN RAISINS

1/4 CUP PINE NUTS,
TOASTED

1/4 CUP SUGAR

1/2 TSP. GROUND
CINNAMON

1/2 TSP. ANCHO CHILE
POWDER

Directions:

1. PREHEAT OVEN TO 350°.
2. MAKE YOUR FAVORITE PIE PASTRY. DIVIDE DOUGH EVENLY INTO 6 BALLS.
3. COVER AND SET ASIDE UNTIL NEEDED.
4. PEEL, CORE AND CHOP APPLES. TOSS WITH LIME JUICE.
5. MELT BUTTER IN SKILLET. ADD APPLES, RAISINS, PINE NUTS, SUGAR AND SPICES.
6. COOK UNTIL APPLES SOFTEN AND BROWN SLIGHTLY. COOL.
7. ROLL DOUGH OUT INTO 6" CIRCLES (ABOUT 3/8" THICK). DIVIDE APPLE MIXTURE ONTO THE BOTTOM HALF OF PIE DOUGH.
8. BRUSH EDGES WITH WATER AND FOLD OVER TO FORM HALF-MOON SHAPED EMPANADAS.
9. CRIMP EDGES WITH A FORK DIPPED IN SUGAR.
10. BRUSH WITH A LITTLE MILK AND BAKE AT 350° FOR ABOUT 20 MINUTES OR UNTIL GOLDEN BROWN AND PUFFED SLIGHTLY.
11. DRIZZLE WITH HONEY OR SERVE WITH ICE CREAM IF DESIRED.
12. BEST SERVED WARM.

ANCHO CHILES

Dried *poblano peppers* that have been left on the plant to ripen until red and then sun dried to a very dark, almost black, color—the main ingredient of Mole Poblano.
(See also Poblano Peppers on pg. 57)

Red Rock Lemonade

SERVES: 6

Directions:

1. CLEAN AND SLICE BERRIES. SPRINKLE WITH SUGAR AND SET ASIDE FOR 20 MINUTES.

2. PLACE LEMON JUICE, SUGARED BERRIES AND GRENADINE IN A BLENDER AND BLEND ON HIGH UNTIL NICELY PURÉED.

3. PLACE INTO A PITCHER WITH WATER AND STIR TO MIX WELL. CHILL.

4. IMMEDIATELY BEFORE SERVING, STIR IN SODA AND RESERVED SLICED BERRIES.

5. WET GLASS EDGES AND DIP INTO SUGAR.

6. FILL PREPARED GLASSES WITH ICE AND LEMONADE. ENJOY.

Note: *Because the sweetness of berries varies during the year, adjust the sugar, lemon and grenadine to taste. You can use frozen berries, again adjusting sugar and grenadine to taste. This is also great when made with fresh or frozen raspberries.*

Ingredients:

1 LB. STRAWBERRIES (RESERVE 6 BERRIES AND SLICE)

1 CUP SUGAR

1 CUP FRESH-SQUEEZED LEMON JUICE (ABOUT 6 LEMONS)

$1/4$ CUP GRENADINE

1 QT. WATER

2 CANS CLUB SODA OR LEMON-LIME SODA, CHILLED

The Birds & The Bees

Springtime, the world around, brings a sense of renewal. After months of colder weather, a warm breeze blows in, the air begins to vibrate with the hum of bees and the return of countless birds. Perhaps it is only natural that we find ourselves with so many reasons to celebrate at this time of the year.

Whether it's a baby shower, a wedding shower, a graduation party or simply a gathering of family and friends, this menu is ideal for any of the various celebrations that seem to be so prevalent in the springtime. It contains some of our favorite appetizers and side dishes including: *Mini Snapper Tostadas, Portabella Mushroom and Spinach Quesadillas, Roasted Corn and Black Bean Salad, Green Chile Macaroni* and *Honey-Chipotle Glazed Chicken Skewers on Fiesta Slaw.* Combine *Sopaipillas with Orange Honey* and *Grand Canyon Margaritas* to create a festive buffet party perfect for celebrating any event in this season of new beginnings.

Mini Snapper Tostadas

Portabella Mushroom &
Spinach Quesadillas

Roasted Corn &
Black Bean Salad

Green Chile Macaroni

Honey-Chipotle Glazed
Chicken Skewers
on Fiesta Slaw

Sopaipillas with Orange Honey

Grand Canyon Margaritas

MINI SNAPPER TOSTADAS

SERVES: 6

Directions:

1. PREHEAT OVEN TO 350°.
2. CUT TORTILLAS INTO 4" ROUNDS OR TRIANGLES. FRY UNTIL CRISP OR SPRAY WITH COOKING SPRAY AND BAKE UNTIL CRISP IN 350° OVEN ABOUT 10 MINUTES.
3. MIX THE BONED AND FLAKED FISH WITH ENOUGH SALSA TO MOISTEN, BUT DO NOT MAKE SOUPY. (SOME TYPES OF FISH WILL USE ALL 12 OZ.) RESERVE ANY LEFTOVER FOR OTHER USE.
4. MASH RIPE AVOCADO WITH SOUR CREAM AND LIME JUICE UNTIL SMOOTH. PUT IN SQUIRT BOTTLE OR ZIPPER-CLOSE PLASTIC BAG. IF USING A BAG, CUT OFF A SMALL PART OF ONE CORNER TO USE LIKE A PASTRY BAG.
5. PLACE CRISP TORTILLA CHIPS ON A PLATTER AND TOP WITH FISH.
6. GARNISH WITH SHREDDED LETTUCE AND SPRINKLE WITH CHEESE.
7. SQUEEZE THE AVOCADO MIXTURE OVER THE TOP AND SERVE QUICKLY TO AVOID SOGGY CHIPS.
8. SERVE WITH ADDITIONAL SALSA FRESCA ON THE SIDE.

See page 45 for Salsa Fresca recipe.

Ingredients:

24 SMALL CORN TORTILLAS (PARTY SIZE OR CUT FROM REGULAR SIZE)

COOKING SPRAY OR OIL FOR FRYING AS NEEDED

2 LBS. BONELESS SNAPPER OR OTHER FLAKY FISH, GRILLED & CHILLED

12 OZ. SALSA FRESCA*

1 MEDIUM AVOCADO

1/2 CUP SOUR CREAM

JUICE FROM 1 LIME

1/2 HEAD ICEBERG LETTUCE, SHREDDED

1/2 CUP COTIJA CHEESE, CRUMBLED

COTIJA CHEESE

A firm, crumbly white Mexican cheese with a flavor similar to Greek Feta but drier and not as salty. Use to crumble on tacos, enchiladas, refried beans and salads. If Cotija is unavailable, Feta cheese can be substituted.

SERVES: 12

PORTABELLA MUSHROOM & SPINACH QUESADILLAS

Ingredients:

3 LBS. PORTABELLA MUSHROOMS

COOKING SPRAY FOR GRILLING

Garlic Butter

2 TBSP. FRESH GARLIC, MINCED

$^1/_2$ CUP BUTTER, SOFTENED

$1^1/_2$ TSP. SHERRY

$1^1/_2$ TSP. WHITE WINE

1 PINCH PARSLEY

1 DASH WHITE PEPPER

6 CUPS SPINACH, WASHED & STEMMED

3 CUPS CHEDDAR CHEESE, SHREDDED

3 CUPS JACK CHEESE, SHREDDED

24 (10") FLOUR TORTILLAS

Directions:

1. PREPARE A MEDIUM-HOT GRILL. TRIM WOODY ENDS FROM THE PORTABELLA STEMS. CLEAN WITH DAMP PAPER TOWELS.

2. LIGHTLY SPRITZ WITH COOKING SPRAY AND PLACE CAP-DOWN ON GRILL. COOK 2-3 MINUTES ON EACH SIDE. COOL AND SLICE.

3. WHIP GARLIC BUTTER INGREDIENTS (GARLIC, BUTTER, SHERRY, WHITE WINE, PARSLEY AND WHITE PEPPER) IN A MIXING BOWL UNTIL FLUFFY.

4. MELT BUTTER IN A SAUCE PAN OVER LOW HEAT.

5. QUICKLY TOSS SPINACH WITH MELTED GARLIC BUTTER IN A LARGE BOWL UNTIL JUST COATED. BE CAREFUL NOT TO COOK THE SPINACH.

6. BLEND THE TWO CHEESES TOGETHER.

7. PLACE 1 TORTILLA ON A HEATED GRIDDLE. TOP WITH $^1/_2$ CUP OF THE CHEESE BLEND, $^1/_2$ CUP GARLIC SPINACH AND THEN $^1/_4$ CUP OF THE GRILLED PORTABELLA MUSHROOMS. TOP WITH ANOTHER TORTILLA.

8. FLIP QUESADILLA WHEN CHEESE BEGINS TO MELT. GRILL UNTIL CRISP ON BOTH SIDES.

9. CUT INTO FOUR PIECES.

10. SERVE WITH GUACAMOLE OR TOMATILLO-AVOCADO SALSA (PAGE 77) ON THE SIDE.

Roasted Corn & Black Bean Salad

Serves: 6

Directions:

1. Roast corn ears in a hot oven for 15 minutes or char on the grill. Cool and cut corn from the ears.

2. In a large bowl, whisk cumin, salt, pepper, sugar, olive oil and vinegar together.

3. Toss in the remaining ingredients and let marinate at least 30 minutes before serving.

4. Stir well before serving. Best when served at room temperature.

Ingredients:

6 ears fresh corn, shucked

Dressing

1 tbsp. ground cumin

1 tbsp. salt

1 tbsp. fresh-ground black pepper

1 tbsp. sugar

1 cup olive oil

1 cup red wine vinegar

2 cups black beans, cooked & rinsed

1 large red bell pepper, 1/2" dice

1 large green bell pepper, 1/2" dice

1 cup red onions, rinsed, 1/4" dice

2-3 jalapeños, minced

4 tbsp. fresh cilantro, chopped

SERVES: 12

GREEN CHILE MACARONI

Ingredients:

Sauce

$^1\!/_2$ CUP BUTTER

$^1\!/_2$ CUP FLOUR

2 CUPS MILK, WARM

2 CUPS GREEN CHILES,*
   ROASTED, PEELED,
   SEEDED & CHOPPED
   (HOT OR MEDIUM,
   ACCORDING TO TASTE)

$^1\!/_2$ TSP. SALT

$^1\!/_2$ TSP. FRESH-GROUND
   BLACK PEPPER

6 CUPS ELBOW MACARONI
   (COOKED AL DENTÉ)

3 CUPS CHEDDAR CHEESE,
   GRATED

Topping

2 CUPS BREAD CRUMBS

2 OZ. BUTTER, MELTED

Directions:

1. PREHEAT OVEN TO 325°.

2. MAKE A WHITE SAUCE BY FIRST MELTING BUTTER AND THEN ADDING FLOUR, STIRRING TO MAKE A ROUX. SLOWLY WHISK IN MILK UNTIL SMOOTH.

3. BRING TO A SIMMER OVER LOW HEAT AND COOK FOR AT LEAST 5 MINUTES TO REMOVE ANY STARCHY TASTE.

4. ADD GREEN CHILES AND SEASON SAUCE WITH SALT AND PEPPER TO TASTE.

5. TOSS MACARONI AND CHEESE IN A BOWL.

6. POUR SAUCE OVER MACARONI AND STIR TO MIX WELL. POUR THE MIXTURE INTO AN OVEN-PROOF BAKING DISH.

7. TOSS THE BREAD CRUMBS WITH MELTED BUTTER AND SPRINKLE OVER THE MACARONI.

8. BAKE UNCOVERED IN A 325° OVEN FOR 30-40 MINUTES OR UNTIL BUBBLY AND NICELY BROWNED.

* Canned green chiles may be substituted.

Honey-Chipotle Glazed Chicken Skewers on Fiesta Slaw

Serves: 6

Directions:

1. Place honey, soy sauce, black pepper, chipotles, lime juice and olive oil in blender.

2. Blend until emulsified. Add salt to taste.

3. Place chicken and half the marinade in a zipper-close plastic bag. Reserve remaining marinade for glazing. Place in refrigerator and marinate for a minimum of 4 hours or overnight.

4. Remove chicken from bag and discard marinade.

5. Take each chicken strip and thread onto the soaked skewers.

6. Grill over a medium-hot grill. After turning once, glaze with remaining marinade on both sides.

7. Place hot skewers on a bed of fiesta slaw to serve.

See page 10 for Fiesta Slaw recipe.

Ingredients:

1/2 cup honey

1/2 cup soy sauce

1 tsp. fresh-ground black pepper

1/4 cup chipotle chiles, canned in adobo sauce

1/4 cup lime juice

1/2 cup olive oil

salt to taste

2 lbs. chicken breasts, cut into strips

12 (10") wooden skewers (soaked in hot water for about an hour)

1 recipe fiesta slaw*

CHIPOTLE CHILES

Jalapeños that have been ripened to red and then dried and smoked over fire. The chiles are sold dry or rehydrated and canned in a rich tomato-vinegar sauce called "Adobo."

YIELD: 36 SOPAIPILLAS

SOPAIPILLAS WITH ORANGE HONEY

Ingredients:

1 PACKET ACTIVE
    DRY YEAST

$1/4$ CUP WARM
    WATER (110°)

1 CUP MILK

1 TBSP. VEGETABLE
    SHORTENING

1 TSP. SALT

2 TSP. SUGAR

3 CUPS ALL PURPOSE
    FLOUR

1 TSP. BAKING POWDER

VEGETABLE OIL
    FOR FRYING

Orange Honey

3 CUPS CLOVER HONEY

$1/4$ CUP ORANGE-BRANDY
    LIQUEUR

POWDERED SUGAR
    AS NEEDED

FRESH BERRIES
    FOR GARNISH

Directions:

1. ADD YEAST TO WARM WATER, STIR TO DISSOLVE AND SET ASIDE FOR 5 MINUTES OR UNTIL FOAMY.

2. BRING MILK TO A BOIL IN A SMALL SAUCEPAN OVER MEDIUM HEAT.

3. REMOVE FROM HEAT AND ADD VEGETABLE SHORTENING, SALT AND SUGAR. LET COOL TO 110°. STIR IN YEAST MIXTURE.

4. SIFT FLOUR AND BAKING POWDER TOGETHER INTO A LARGE BOWL. POUR THE WET INGREDIENTS INTO THE DRY AND STIR UNTIL THE DOUGH IS MOIST. TURN OUT ONTO A LIGHTLY FLOURED BOARD AND KNEAD UNTIL SMOOTH AND ELASTIC (APPROX. 10 MINUTES). COVER THE DOUGH WITH A CLOTH TOWEL AND LET SIT FOR 20 MINUTES.

5. ON A LIGHTLY FLOURED BOARD, ROLL OUT DOUGH TO A $1/4$" THICKNESS AND CUT INTO TRIANGLES OR SQUARES ABOUT 3 INCHES ACROSS.

6. POUR ENOUGH OIL INTO A LARGE, HEAVY BOTTOM SAUCEPAN TO A DEPTH OF 3". HEAT OIL OVER HIGH HEAT UNTIL IT REACHES 400°.

7. FRY SOPAIPILLAS IN THE HOT OIL UNTIL GOLDEN BROWN ON BOTH SIDES. DRAIN ON PAPER TOWELS.

8. WHISK HONEY AND ORANGE-BRANDY LIQUEUR TOGETHER IN A SMALL BOWL. SET OVER HOT WATER TO THIN AND WARM.

9. WHEN ALL SOPAIPILLAS ARE DONE, DUST WITH POWDERED SUGAR, DRIZZLE WITH THE ORANGE HONEY AND GARNISH WITH FRESH BERRIES. SERVE IMMEDIATELY.

GRAND CANYON MARGARITAS

SERVES: 12

Directions:

1. MIX FROZEN CONCENTRATES WITH WATER.
2. ADD REMAINING INGREDIENTS AND STIR WELL.
3. ADJUST TEQUILA STRENGTH TO TASTE.
4. SERVE WELL-CHILLED IN SALT-RIMMED GLASSES OR ON THE ROCKS.

Ingredients:

2 CANS (10 OZ.) FROZEN LIMEADE CONCENTRATE

2 CANS (10 OZ.) FROZEN LEMONADE CONCENTRATE

1 GALLON WATER

1 LITRE GOLD TEQUILA

2 CUPS TRIPLE SEC

$1/2$ CUP PRICKLY PEAR SYRUP

$1/2$ CUP CRANBERRY JUICE

2 CUPS FRESH-SQUEEZED ORANGE JUICE

1 CUP FRESH-SQUEEZED LIME JUICE

South Texas Tortilla Soup

Yucatan Orange-Jicama Salad
with Pomegranates

Pork Tenderloin with Chorizo Gravy

Southwest Scalloped Potatoes

Molten Mocha Cake

Just Among Friends

Every season offers opportunities to have a few special people over for dinner. This meal is perfect for those crisp spring evenings when you still need a sweater after the sun goes down.

Our *South Texas Tortilla Soup* is a warming first course that makes enough to have some left for lunch the next day. The intriguing textures and flavors of our refreshing *Yucatan Orange-Jicama Salad* combine with the *Pork Tenderloin with Chorizo Gravy* and *Southwest Scalloped Potatoes* to make a delicious and hearty meal.

Of course for us, no evening is complete without chocolate— one of our favorites, *Molten Mocha Cake,* makes even simple occasions end like a feast.

SOUTH TEXAS TORTILLA SOUP

Directions:

1. IN LARGE KETTLE, HEAT OIL AND ADD PEPPERS, ONIONS, POBLANOS AND GARLIC. COOK 2-3 MINUTES OR UNTIL ONIONS BEGIN TO TURN TRANSLUCENT.

2. TEAR CORN TORTILLAS INTO THIN STRIPS AND ADD TO VEGETABLES. STIR UNTIL TORTILLAS BEGIN TO SOFTEN. ADD SPICES AND MIX WELL.

3. ADD STOCK AND TOMATOES. BRING TO A BOIL.

4. SIMMER FOR 20 MINUTES, STIRRING OFTEN TO AVOID SCORCHING.

5. TASTE AND ADJUST SEASONINGS IF NECESSARY. STIR IN HALF OF CILANTRO (FROM GARNISHES).

6. IF USING, ADD OPTIONAL SEAFOOD OR CHICKEN*. HEAT THROUGH AND SERVE.

7. GARNISH WITH CRISP TORTILLA CHIPS, CHEESE AND CILANTRO.

   Optional: For a more hearty soup, add 2 lbs. cooked, diced chicken or mixed seafood.

   Note: After completely chilling, this soup can be frozen in plastic freezer bags. Add the optional protein only when re-heating. Do not add before freezing.

QUESO FRESCO

A fresh, unaged cows' milk from Mexico with a mild, creamy flavor. It is usually packed in whey and crumbles well.

Ingredients:

Soup Base
2 TBSP. OLIVE OIL

2 GREEN BELL PEPPERS, DICED

1 LARGE ONION, DICED

4 POBLANO CHILES, SEEDED & DICED

3 CLOVES FRESH GARLIC, MINCED

12 CORN TORTILLAS, CUT OR TORN INTO STRIPS

1 TBSP. GROUND CUMIN

1 1/2 TSP. FRESH-GROUND BLACK PEPPER

1 1/2 TSP. OREGANO

1 TBSP. NEW MEXICAN RED CHILE POWDER

4 QTS. STRONG CHICKEN STOCK (OR CHICKEN BOUILLON/WATER)

3 CANS (14 OZ.) DICED TOMATOES, UNDRAINED

1 CAN (14 OZ.) PUREED TOMATOES

Garnishes
1/2 LB. CRISP TORTILLA CHIPS, STRIPS OR CRUMBLES)

1 LB. QUESO FRESCO OR JACK CHEESE, SHREDDED

1 BUNCH CILANTRO, WASHED & FINELY CHOPPED

SERVES: 6

YUCATAN ORANGE-JICAMA SALAD WITH POMEGRANATES

Ingredients:

Vinaigrette

1 CUP FRESH-SQUEEZED
    ORANGE JUICE

1 TBSP. ORANGE ZEST

1/2 CUP RICE VINEGAR

3 TBSP. SUGAR

1/2 TSP. FRESH-GROUND
    BLACK PEPPER

1 TSP. SALT

2 CUPS VEGETABLE OIL

2 TSP. FRESH CILANTRO,
    CHOPPED

Salad

3 CUPS JICAMA,
    PEELED & JULIENNED

4 LARGE ORANGES,
    PEELED, SEEDED &
    CUT IN SEGMENTS

3 CUPS MIXED GREENS

6 ROMA TOMATOES,
    QUARTERED

1 CUP FRESH
    POMEGRANATE SEEDS

Directions:

1. WHISK ALL VINAIGRETTE INGREDIENTS TOGETHER EXCEPT
   OIL AND CILANTRO. WHEN SUGAR AND SALT ARE DISSOLVED,
   SLOWLY WHISK IN OIL UNTIL THE DRESSING IS EMULSIFIED.
   ADD THE CILANTRO.

2. IN A LARGE BOWL, GENTLY TOSS JICAMA, ORANGES AND
   MIXED GREENS WITH ABOUT 1/2 CUP OF DRESSING.

3. CUT POMEGRANATE IN HALF AND PICK OUT THE FLESHY,
   EDIBLE SEEDS (MEAT) WITH A FORK, BEING CAREFUL NOT
   TO PUNCTURE.

4. ARRANGE SALAD ON 6 CHILLED PLATES AND GARNISH WITH
   ROMA TOMATO WEDGES.

5. SPRINKLE WITH POMEGRANATE SEEDS. PASS REMAINING
   DRESSING IN A PRETTY BOWL OR PITCHER TO DRIZZLE
   OVER SALADS.

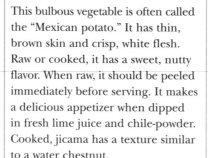

JICAMA

This bulbous vegetable is often called
the "Mexican potato." It has thin,
brown skin and crisp, white flesh.
Raw or cooked, it has a sweet, nutty
flavor. When raw, it should be peeled
immediately before serving. It makes
a delicious appetizer when dipped
in fresh lime juice and chile-powder.
Cooked, jicama has a texture similar
to a water chestnut.

Pork Tenderloin with Chorizo Gravy

Serves: 6

Directions:

1. Make marinade by chopping chiles into a paste. Place in a zipper-close plastic bag with olive oil, salt, pepper and lime juice.
2. Clean tenderloin of any fat or silver skin. Add to marinade. Refrigerate for a minimum of 4 hours or overnight.
3. Brown chorizo over medium heat and place in a strainer to drain excess fat. Set aside.
4. Heat milk and cream with garlic. Simmer 10 minutes.
5. Strain out garlic and add chorizo to mixture. Simmer 15-20 minutes or until slightly thickened. Keep warm until served.
6. Remove pork from bag and discard marinade.
7. Cook on a hot grill for about 8 minutes, turning several times to cook evenly.
8. Let rest 5 minutes then carve into 1/2" thick slices.
9. Divide into 6 servings and serve with gravy ladled over top.

Ingredients:

Marinade
2 TBSP. CHIPOTLE PEPPERS, CANNED IN ADOBO SAUCE

1/4 CUP OLIVE OIL

1 TSP. SALT

1 TSP. FRESH-GROUND BLACK PEPPER

2 TBSP. LIME JUICE

3 LBS. PORK TENDERLOIN

Gravy
1 LB. PORK CHORIZO

1 CUP MILK

1 CUP HEAVY CREAM

6 CLOVES GARLIC, LIGHTLY CRUSHED

Chorizo

Mexican chorizo is a sausage typically made of pork, chile, paprika and salt. Many brands are available, raw or smoked, made with pork, beef, or turkey. If using uncooked, cook and drain off the oil before using in egg dishes. Chorizos can vary in heat from mild to wild. They can be found in natural casings or in plastic sleeves.

25

SERVES: 6

SOUTHWEST SCALLOPED POTATOES

Ingredients:

2 LBS. RUSSET POTATOES, THINLY SLICED

4 BABY RED POTATOES, THICKLY SLICED

1 CUP HEAVY CREAM

1 TBSP. GROUND CUMIN, TOASTED

1 TBSP. GARLIC SALT

1 TBSP. SALT

2 TSP. FRESH-GROUND BLACK PEPPER

3 TBSP. FRESH CILANTRO, CHOPPED

1 CUP RED ONIONS, THINLY SLICED

3 GREEN ONIONS, CHOPPED

1 LARGE POBLANO PEPPER, ROASTED, PEELED, SEEDED & CHOPPED

12 CORN TORTILLAS

$1/4$ CUP OLIVE OIL

4 TBSP. BUTTER

Directions:

1. PREHEAT OVEN TO 350°.
2. COMBINE AND BLANCH POTATOES IN BOILING WATER FOR 2-3 MINUTES. DRAIN WELL.
3. TOSS POTATOES WITH CREAM AND SEASONINGS.
4. MIX ONIONS TOGETHER WITH POBLANO PEPPER.
5. HEAT OIL IN A CAST IRON SKILLET OR OTHER OVEN-PROOF DISH. REMOVE FROM HEAT.
6. MAKE A LAYER OF POTATOES IN THE BOTTOM OF THE DISH IN A CIRCULAR PATTERN.
7. TOP THIS WITH A LAYER OF ONIONS AND PEPPERS.
8. CUT 8 TORTILLAS INTO THIN STRIPS. DIVIDE HALF OVER THIS LAYER.
9. MAKE ANOTHER LAYER OF POTATOES, ONION MIXTURE AND TORTILLAS.
10. END WITH A LAYER OF POTATOES.
11. MELT BUTTER. USING A FOOD PROCESSOR, CHOP REMAINING 4 TORTILLAS INTO COARSE CRUMBS. MIX WITH BUTTER.
12. SPRINKLE BUTTERED CRUMBS OVER POTATOES.
13. PLACE IN 350° OVEN AND BAKE FOR ONE HOUR OR UNTIL POTATOES ARE TENDER AND NICELY BROWNED.

MOLTEN MOCHA CAKE

SERVES: 6

Directions:

1. PREHEAT OVEN TO 350°.
2. BUTTER SIX (6 OZ.) RAMEKINS. RESERVE.

Sauce

1. OVER MEDIUM HEAT COMBINE WATER, COCOA POWDER, BUTTER AND CHOCOLATE CHIPS IN A DOUBLE BOILER. HEAT UNTIL CHIPS AND BUTTER MELT, STIRRING WELL TO MIX.
2. WHIP IN REMAINING SAUCE INGREDIENTS UNTIL SMOOTH AND DIVIDE INTO THE SIX RAMEKINS.

Cakes

1. OVER MEDIUM HEAT, MELT BUTTER AND CHOCOLATE TOGETHER IN A DOUBLE BOILER.
2. MEANWHILE, WHIP EGGS WITH SUGAR IN A MIXER UNTIL LIGHT AND FLUFFY. SPRINKLE FLOUR OVER THE TOP AND MIX UNTIL JUST INCORPORATED.
3. REMOVE CHOCOLATE FROM HEAT WHEN MELTED. COOL SLIGHTLY AND STIR INTO THE EGG MIXTURE.
4. SPOON INTO PREPARED RAMEKINS ON TOP OF SAUCE.
5. BAKE IN 350° OVEN IN A WATER BATH FOR ABOUT 15-20 MINUTES. CAKES WILL STILL BE RUNNY IN THE CENTER.
6. REMOVE FROM OVEN AND LET REST 5 MINUTES.
7. TURN OUT ONTO SERVING PLATES AND GARNISH WITH A LITTLE WHIPPED CREAM IF DESIRED.

> *Note:* The sauce should flow over the cakes and more will come out when cut open with a fork.

Ingredients:

Sauce

1/3 CUP WATER

2 TBSP. COCOA POWDER

1/2 STICK BUTTER

3 OZ. SEMI-SWEET CHOCOLATE CHIPS

2 TBSP. LIGHT CORN SYRUP

2 TBSP. COFFEE LIQUEUR

1/3 CUP SUGAR

Cakes

2 STICKS UNSALTED BUTTER

12 OZ. SEMI-SWEET CHOCOLATE CHIPS

6 LARGE EGGS

1 CUP SUGAR

1/2 CUP FLOUR

Three Sisters

During this season of planting and new growth, we celebrate the "three sister" staple foods of the American Southwest's indigenous peoples—corn, beans and squash. When planted in the same hill, they grow together with the strong corn stalks acting as a natural trellis to support the bean and squash vines. In the same way, the combination of these three foods can alone sustain an entire community.

This meal incorporates these "three sisters" with other delicious ingredients. The *Smoked Trout and Bean Salad* drizzled with *Avocado Crema* is a delightful appetizer. The flavors of the *Corn and Green Chile Tamales* and *Grilled Vegetable Salsa* meld with the *Orange and Red Grape Salad* to make the perfect meal for that first Spring dinner on the patio.

Smoked Trout &
Bean Salad with
Avocado Crema

Corn & Green Chile
Tamales with
Grilled Vegetable Salsa

Orange & Red Grape
Salad with Prickly Pear
Vinaigrette

SMOKED TROUT & BEAN SALAD WITH AVOCADO CREMA

SERVES: 6

Directions:

Avocado Crema

1. IN A BLENDER, COMBINE ALL INGREDIENTS. BLEND UNTIL WELL MIXED. RESERVE.

Salad

1. REMOVE TROUT FROM SKINS AND CRUMBLE.

2. MIX TROUT WITH CORN, PEPPERS, BEANS, SCALLIONS, CILANTRO, GARLIC SALT AND PEPPER.

3. WHEN WELL MIXED, ADD IN THE MAYONNAISE.

4. CHILL WELL.

5. FILL LETTUCE CUPS WITH TROUT AND BEAN SALAD. DRIZZLE WITH AVOCADO CREMA.

7. SERVE IMMEDIATELY.

Canned beans which have been rinsed and drained can be substituted.

Ingredients:

Avocado Crema

1 RIPE AVOCADO

$3/4$ CUP MAYONNAISE OR SOUR CREAM

JUICE FROM 1 LIME

Salad

$1 1/2$ CUPS SMOKED TROUT (ABOUT 3 SKIN-ON FILLETS)

$3/4$ CUP FRESH CORN, ROASTED

$3/4$ CUP RED BELL PEPPERS, $1/4$" DICE

1 CUP COOKED WHITE, PINTO OR BLACK BEANS,* RINSED

$3/4$ CUP SCALLIONS, VERY THINLY SLICED

$1/4$ CUP FRESH CILANTRO, WELL WASHED & CHOPPED

$1/4$ TSP. GARLIC SALT

$1/2$ TSP. FRESH-GROUND BLACK PEPPER

6 TBSP. MAYONNAISE

6 LEAVES ICEBERG LETTUCE, TRIMMED TO MAKE ROUND CUPS

SERVES: 6

CORN & GREEN CHILE TAMALES WITH GRILLED VEGETABLE SALSA

Ingredients:

2 LBS. PREPARED MASA

12 OZ. VEGETABLE
    SHORTENING
    (OR BUTTER)

1 TBSP. BAKING POWDER

1 TBSP. SALT
    (OR TO TASTE)

3 FRESH EARS CORN,
    CORN CUT OFF AND
    COB SCRAPED

12 LARGE DRIED
    CORN HUSKS

4 OZ. CANNED WHOLE
    GREEN CHILES,
    CUT INTO STRIPS

6 (1 OZ.) CHEDDAR CHEESE
    STICKS, 1/2" X 3"
    (OPTIONAL)

Directions:

1. MIX MASA WITH SHORTENING AND BAKING POWDER IN A LARGE BOWL OR MIXER. WHIP FOR 8-10 MINUTES OR UNTIL VERY LIGHT AND FLUFFY. ADD SALT, THEN PINCH OFF A SMALL AMOUNT AND COOK IN A SKILLET TO TASTE FOR SALTINESS. ADJUST SALT IF NECESSARY. ADD CORN AND SCRAPINGS. COVER AND LET REST FOR 30 MINUTES.

2. WHILE MASA IS RESTING, SOAK CORN HUSKS IN HOT WATER UNTIL SOFTENED. DRAIN AND PAT DRY.

3. DIVIDE MASA EVENLY ONTO 12 LARGE HUSKS (ABOUT 1 CUP EACH) AND SPREAD TO EDGES.

4. PLACE GREEN CHILE STRIPS DOWN THE MIDDLE OF THE MASA AND, IF USING, PLACE THE CHEESE STICKS ON TOP OF THE CHILES.

5. ROLL HUSK LIKE A CIGAR, SEALING MASA OVER FILLING BY PINCHING THE ENDS. TUCK HUSK ENDS UNDER, SO THEY OVERLAP IN THE CENTER AND TIE THE TAMALE WITH A STRIP OF HUSK. REFRIGERATE.

MASA & MASA HARINA

Fresh prepared Masa is corn that has been soaked in slabbed lime water and then ground to form a moist thick dough. Masa Harina is a corn meal made from dehydrated Masa that has been ground very fine. If fresh Masa is unavailable use Masa Harina mixed 50/50 with water and proceed as above.

To Serve

1. STEAM TAMALES FOR 30-45 MINUTES OVER MEDIUM HEAT. TAMALES ARE DONE WHEN MASA PULLS EASILY AWAY FROM THE HUSK.

2. SERVE WITH HUSKS OPENED AND GRILLED VEGETABLE SALSA (PAGE 31) SPOONED OVER THE TOP.

CORN & GREEN CHILE TAMALES WITH GRILLED VEGETABLE SALSA (CONT.)

SERVES: 6

Directions:

Grilled Vegetable Salsa

1. SEASON ZUCCHINI, TOMATOES AND ONION WITH 1 TBSP. OF OLIVE OIL AND 1 TBSP. OF BALSAMIC VINEGAR. LIGHTLY GRILL JUST UNTIL MARKED ON BOTH SIDES, BUT STILL CRISP. (CORN WILL TAKE ABOUT 6 MINUTES.) COOL.

2. CUT CORN FROM COB. DICE ZUCCHINI, TOMATOES AND ONIONS INTO 1/2" PIECES. TOSS TOGETHER.

3. MINCE SERRANO CHILES AND DICE ROASTED RED BELL PEPPER. ADD TO SALSA.

4. SEASON WITH REMAINING OLIVE OIL AND BALSAMIC VINEGAR. ADD SALT AND PEPPER TO TASTE. TOSS IN CILANTRO OR BASIL.

Ingredients:

Grilled Vegetable Salsa

2 MEDIUM ZUCCHINI, SLICED LENGTHWISE— 1/2" THICK

4 LARGE ROMA TOMATOES, SLICED IN HALF

1 LARGE RED ONION, SLICED—1/2" THICK

2 TBSP. OLIVE OIL

2 TBSP. BALSAMIC VINEGAR (OR TO TASTE)

1 EAR OF CORN, GRILL WITHOUT HUSKS

1-2 MEDIUM SERRANO CHILES (OR TO TASTE)

1 LARGE RED BELL PEPPER, ROASTED, SEEDED & PEELED

SALT & PEPPER TO TASTE

1-2 TBSP. FRESH CILANTRO OR BASIL, CHOPPED (OR TO TASTE)

SERRANO CHILES

Slender, light-green chile peppers, usually 1 1/2" to 3" long. Can pack a punch! Considered to be medium-hot. Use seeds and all—sparingly. Has a very clean, fresh taste.

ROASTING & GRILLING VEGETABLES

American Southwest cuisine relies heavily on vegetables. We believe that the types of vegetables and how they are prepared are one key to creating an excellent meal.

Potatoes are long-time favorites for roasting, but many other root vegetables, including beets, carrots, turnips and parsnips are classic candidates for roasting, as are zucchini, mushrooms, asparagus and fennel. To roast any vegetable, coat with butter or good-quality oil to seal in the moisture, place in a single layer in an oven-proof dish. Cook at high temperature in a dry heat oven. Do not add additional liquids or the vegetables will glaze rather than roast.

With the popularity of grilling meats, especially in the summer, it only makes sense to prepare vegetables the same way. For the most part, vegetables are easily seasoned for the grill with a little good oil, salt and pepper, or a simple marinade. However, there are a few preparation tips for successfully grilling different types of vegetables.

Vegetables such as whole corn, asparagus, small to medium mushrooms and green onions can be grilled in their whole form. Others, including fennel, baby artichokes, squashes, zucchini and eggplant should be cut into $1/2$" to $3/4$" thick slices. Be careful not to slice too thin or they may slide through the grates of the grill. Also be careful not to overcook as these vegetables tend to cook very quickly. Potatoes, Brussels sprouts, large artichokes and carrots can also be grilled if they are first blanched until just tender. Since these are already cooked, grilling these enhances flavor and appearance. You can also add flare to your meal by combining many of these varieties to create grilled vegetable skewers.

Have fun experimenting with roasting and grilling "new" vegetables. You may discover new favorites and learn to enjoy the enhanced flavors and colors that these methods can provide.

Orange & Red Grape Salad with Prickly Pear Vinaigrette

SERVES: 6

Directions:

Vinaigrette

* If lucky enough to find the fresh fruit, cut out the thorns and peel. Purée, then strain to remove seeds.

1. IN A BLENDER, ADD PRICKLY PEAR SYRUP (OR FRESH FRUIT PURÉE), ORANGE JUICE, GARLIC, CAYENNE, SALT AND VINEGAR.

2. WITH BLENDER RUNNING, SLOWLY DRIZZLE IN OIL UNTIL EMULSIFIED. CHILL UNTIL READY TO USE.

Salad

1. ARRANGE GREENS AROUND A DECORATIVE PLATTER.

2. SLICE ORANGES INTO $1/4$" SLICES AND ARRANGE ON GREENS.

3. SCATTER GRAPES OVER THE SALAD AND DRIZZLE WITH ABOUT 1 CUP OF VINAIGRETTE.

Ingredients:

Vinaigrette

$1/4$ CUP PRICKLY PEAR SYRUP (OR FRESH PRICKLY PEAR FRUIT*)

$1/4$ CUP ORANGE JUICE

1 CLOVE FRESH GARLIC, PEELED

1 PINCH CAYENNE PEPPER

$1/4$ TSP. SALT (OR TO TASTE)

2 TBSP. RICE VINEGAR

$2/3$ CUP VEGETABLE OIL

Salad

4 CUPS SPINACH, WASHED & STEMMED

6 LARGE SEEDLESS ORANGES, PEELED AND PITH REMOVED

2 CUPS RED GRAPES, CUT IN HALF

PRICKLY PEARS

A flat leafed cacti that produces beautiful flowers and very sweet fruit that is usually used to flavor drinks, vinaigrettes, jellies and candies. The fresh fruits are available seasonally and are best prepared by peeling off the skin and thorns, chopping or pureeing the flesh and then straining to remove the seeds. Bottled juice/syrup can be found year-round at specialty stores. The young pads are known as *Nopalitos* and taste somewhat like green beans.

33

Sonoran Summer Solstice
Brunch in the Garden
Star Gazing Party
Late Summer Rain

Summer

Black Bean Sopes with Cotija Cheese
& Grilled Cactus Salsa

Mahi Mahi with Coconut Rice
& Grilled Pineapple Salsa

Chocolate Cinnamon Shortbreads
with Fresh Berries

Sonoran Summer Solstice

Midsummer's Night has always seemed like a magical time, especially in one of the most beautiful stretches of the Southwest—Arizona's Sonora Desert. Here the solstice is celebrated by roadrunners, lizards, tortoises and other desert-loving creatures who make their homes among the rocks, saguaro cactus and palo verde trees.

This meal is ideal for Summer's hottest days. The delightfully savory *Black Bean Sopes with Cotija Cheese* and our favorite *Grilled Cactus Salsa*, are a prelude to the fresh *Mahi Mahi with Grilled Pineapple Salsa* on its bed of savory-sweet *Coconut Rice*. The *Chocolate Cinnamon Shortbreads with Fresh Berries* allow you to make the most of the season's abundance with a simple, yet decadent dessert.

Black Bean Sopes with Cotija Cheese

Yields: 18 pieces

Directions:

Masa
1. Mix masa harina and water together, until a soft dough forms. Let rest 30 minutes.
2. Divide masa into 18 balls, making sure the dough stays covered by a wet towel to avoid drying.
3. Press portions by hand into a 2" circle. Pinch up a rim around the top of each to form the sope.
4. Place 2 tbsp. oil in a hot skillet and fry 2-3 minutes on each side, or until lightly browned and puffy.
5. Drain well on paper towels and keep warm in oven.

Filling
1. Heat 3 tbsp. of oil in a skillet.
2. Add onions to skillet and cook until translucent.
3. Add black beans and smash into a coarse puree with the back of a spoon or potato masher. If mixture seems too dry, add a little reserved bean juice.
4. Fry this mixture for 2-3 minutes.
5. Stir in cumin, garlic and salt. Mix well
6. Fry this mixture until the beans begin to become crisp on the outside, stirring this crust back into the beans. Be careful not to scorch.

Assembly
1. Place prepared sopes on a baking sheet.
2. Top each with some of the refried black beans and sprinkle with cotija cheese. Heat in oven until hot and serve immediately. Garnish with grilled cactus salsa (page 38).

* Canned beans which have been rinsed and drained can be substituted, reserving some of the liquid.

Ingredients:

Masa
2 cups masa harina
1 1/2 cups warm water
2 tbsp. vegetable oil

Filling
3 tbsp. vegetable oil
1/4 cup yellow onion, finely diced
3 cups cooked black beans* (reserve bean juice)
1 tsp. ground cumin
1 tsp. fresh garlic, minced
1/2 tsp. salt (or to taste)
4 oz. cotija cheese, crumbled

SERVES: 6

GRILLED CACTUS SALSA & GRILLED PINEAPPLE SALSA

Ingredients:

Grilled Cactus Salsa
4 MEDIUM CACTUS PADS
1 LB. ROMA TOMATOES
OLIVE OIL FOR GRILLING
1 CUCUMBER, PEELED
  & SEEDED
1 CUP RED ONIONS,
  FINELY DICED
$1/2$ CUP CILANTRO,
  CHOPPED
2 TBSP FRESH SAGE,
  CHOPPED
1 TSP. CUMIN, TOASTED
1 TBSP. GARLIC, MINCED
1 TSP. SALT
$1/2$ TSP. FRESH-GROUND
  BLACK PEPPER
$1/4$ CUP OLIVE OIL
1 JALAPEÑOS, MINCED
2 TBSP. LIME JUICE
2 OZ. MESCAL OR TEQUILA

Grilled Pineapple Salsa
1 WHOLE PINEAPPLE
$1/2$ CUP RED BELL
  PEPPER, $1/4$" DICE
$1/2$ CUP GREEN BELL
  PEPPER, $1/4$" DICE
4 TBSP. FRESH CILANTRO,
  ROUGHLY CHOPPED
$1/2$ TSP. SALT
$1/4$ TSP. RED CHILE FLAKES
4 TSP. SUGAR
$1/4$ CUP RICE VINEGAR

Directions:

Grilled Cactus Salsa
1. PREPARE CACTUS PADS BY CAREFULLY CUTTING OUT THE THORNY "EYES" WITH A PARING KNIFE AND PEELING OFF THE SKIN.
2. BRUSH TOMATOES AND CACTUS PADS WITH A LITTLE OLIVE OIL.
3. GRILL OR BROIL UNTIL TOMATOES ARE SLIGHTLY BLACKENED AND CACTUS PADS BEGIN TO SOFTEN.
4. PLACE CUCUMBER AND GRILLED TOMATOES IN FOOD PROCESSOR AND PROCESS TO A RATHER COARSE PURÉE. POUR INTO A MIXING BOWL.
5. DICE CACTUS PADS $1/8$" X $1/8$" AND ADD TO PURÉE.
6. ADD ALL REMAINING INGREDIENTS, MIXING WELL, AND REFRIGERATE AT LEAST 4 HOURS OR OVERNIGHT.
7. LET COME ALMOST TO ROOM TEMPERATURE. TASTE AND ADJUST SEASONINGS IF NECESSARY.
8. SERVE WITH BLACK BEAN SOPES (PAGE 37). ALSO GREAT SERVED WITH CHIPS, WARM WHITE CHEESE QUESADILLAS OR GRILLED MEATS.

Grilled Pineapple Salsa
1. PEEL AND SLICE PINEAPPLE, CORING IF NECESSARY.
2. LIGHTLY OIL A GRILL AND COOK PINEAPPLE SLICES UNTIL LIGHTLY GRILLED ON BOTH SIDES AND SMELLING WONDERFUL. COOL.
3. DICE PINEAPPLE SLICES AND TOSS IN A BOWL WITH REMAINING INGREDIENTS.
4. LET REST 30 MINUTES BEFORE USING.
5. BEST SERVED AT ROOM TEMPERATURE. SERVE WITH MAHI MAHI (PAGE 40).

MARINADES & RUBS

Marinades and rubs are integral to creating the American Southwest flavor. Typically these treatments are used to enhance flavor and to tenderize meats before cooking. The vinegars and soy sauces in marinades provide acidity and salinity, which act as tenderizing agents. The combinations of herbs and spices in both methods offer nearly endless flavor varieties and textures.

Marinades are combinations of herbs and spices, usually in a base of vinegar, citrus juice, alcohol or soy sauce. Primarily marinades are used to add flavor, but sometimes it is necessary to use them for longer periods of time to tenderize meat. If this is the case, be careful not to leave meat in a marinade for longer than 24 hours or the meat will begin to "cure"—cook without heat. Although sometimes this is the desired result, for most roasting and grilling purposes, curing is not preferable.

Rubs are dry or wet pastes of herbs, spices and often a sugar or sweet component. They utilize many of the same principles as marinades and are applied to the outside of meats before roasting, grilling or baking to develop a crisp external crust. Rubs generally can be applied for longer periods of time than marinades, but will also have a curing effect if left for too long.

While our recipes offer specific flavor combinations, don't be afraid to experiment with rubs and marinades. Although lamb and rosemary, chicken and thyme, and salmon and dill are classic combinations, use these as a starting point for your own creations. These methods provide nearly limitless opportunities to perfect recipes to your own tastes.

SERVES: 6

MAHI MAHI WITH COCONUT RICE

Ingredients:

Marinade

1/2 CUP RICE VINEGAR

4 GREEN ONIONS, FINELY CHOPPED

2 TSP. DIJON MUSTARD

1/2 TSP. CRUSHED DRIED RED PEPPER

3 TBSP. OLIVE OIL

6 (8 OZ.) MAHI MAHI FILLETS, 1/2" - 3/4" THICK, SKIN-OFF

Coconut Rice

4 CUPS WATER

1 CAN (14 OZ.) THAI STYLE, UNSWEETENED COCONUT MILK

1-2 TBSP. THAI STYLE, SRIRACHA/ROOSTER CHILE-GARLIC SAUCE

1 TSP. SALT

1 CUP CRUSHED PINEAPPLE, IN JUICE

3 CUPS CONVERTED RICE

Directions:

Mahi Mahi

1. IN A SHALLOW BOWL COMBINE VINEGAR, ONIONS, MUSTARD AND PEPPER.

2. WHISK IN OLIVE OIL, A LITTLE AT A TIME, UNTIL WELL BLENDED.

3. PLACE IN A LARGE ZIPPER-CLOSE PLASTIC BAG AND ADD FILLETS. MARINATE FOR 1-4 HOURS, REFRIGERATED, TURNING OCCASIONALLY.

4. PREHEAT A BROILER OR GRILL TO MEDIUM HOT.

5. REMOVE MAHI MAHI FROM THE REFRIGERATOR 30 MINUTES BEFORE COOKING.

6. REMOVE FISH FROM BAG AND DISCARD MARINADE.

7. GRILL THE FISH 4-5 MINUTES PER SIDE OR UNTIL JUST BEGINNING TO FLAKE.

Coconut Rice

1. COMBINE WATER, COCONUT MILK, CHILE SAUCE, SALT AND PINEAPPLE WITH JUICE IN A SAUCE PAN OVER HIGH HEAT. STIR TO MIX.

2. ADD RICE AND BRING TO A BOIL.

3. REDUCE HEAT AND COVER. SIMMER UNDISTURBED FOR ABOUT 15-20 MINUTES.

4. UNCOVER AND TEST FOR TENDERNESS. WHEN TENDER, COVER TIGHTLY, REMOVE FROM HEAT AND LET REST FOR 5-10 MINUTES. FLUFF RICE WITH A FORK.

To Serve:

MAKE A BED OF RICE ON EACH PLATE. PLACE MAHI MAHI FILLET ON THE RICE AND GARNISH WITH GRILLED PINEAPPLE SALSA (PAGE 38).

CHOCOLATE CINNAMON SHORTBREADS WITH FRESH BERRIES

Directions:

Shortbreads

1. IN A MEDIUM BOWL WITH AN ELECTRIC MIXER, BEAT TOGETHER BUTTER, SUGAR AND CINNAMON UNTIL THE MIXTURE IS LIGHT AND FLUFFY.

2. ADD EGG YOLK AND MIX WELL.

3. MIX FLOUR WITH COCOA AND SALT. STIR THIS INTO SUGAR MIXTURE UNTIL INCORPORATED. IF THE DOUGH FEELS TOO SOFT, ADD MORE FLOUR, A LITTLE AT A TIME.

4. SHAPE THE DOUGH INTO A LOG ABOUT 3" IN DIAMETER AND WRAP TIGHTLY IN A PLASTIC WRAP. REFRIGERATE FOR AT LEAST 2 HOURS.

5. PREHEAT OVEN TO 350°. LIGHTLY BUTTER A BAKING SHEET. UNWRAP THE REFRIGERATED DOUGH AND CUT INTO 1/2" SLICES.

6. PLACE ON BAKING SHEET AND BAKE FOR 15 MINUTES OR UNTIL LIGHT BROWN.

Topping

1. MIX SUGAR, CINNAMON AND COCOA POWDER IN A SHALLOW PLATE OR BOWL. WHILE THE COOKIES ARE STILL WARM, ROLL THEM IN THIS MIXTURE AND TRANSFER TO A COOLING RACK.

Sauce

1. PURÉE 1/2 CUP OF STRAWBERRIES WITH SUGAR. PLACE IN A BOWL WITH REMAINING SLICED STRAWBERRIES.

2. TO SERVE: LACE THE SHORTBREADS ON SERVING PLATES. LADLE STRAWBERRY SAUCE ON HALF OF EACH SHORTBREAD AND GARNISH WITH FRESH RASPBERRIES.

3. ADD A SCOOP OF YOUR FAVORITE VANILLA ICE CREAM.

Ingredients:

Shortbreads

1/4 CUP UNSALTED BUTTER, SOFTENED

1/2 CUP SUGAR

2 TSP. GROUND CINNAMON

1 EGG YOLK, ROOM TEMPERATURE

1/2 CUP ALL PURPOSE FLOUR

1 TBSP. COCOA POWDER

1 PINCH SALT

Topping

2 TBSP. SUGAR

1 TSP. CINNAMON

1 TSP. COCOA POWDER

Sauce

1 CUP FRESH STRAWBERRIES, SLICED

1/2 CUP SUGAR

1/2 CUP FRESH RASPBERRIES

Rocky Pointe Shrimp Cocktail

Pecan-Crusted Crab Cakes
with Chipotle Remoulade

Chorizo, Egg & Potato Tacos
with Salsa Fresca

Nopalitos, Shrimp & Cherry Tomato
Salad with Chile-Lime Vinaigrette

Tres Leches Cake with Marinated Fruit

Brunch in the Garden

There is nothing quite so welcoming as a table set in the heart of a Summer garden. With colorful napkins and a pitcher of fresh-cut flowers, guests will be able to enjoy that wonderful time of day when the dew has dried from the grass, but the Summer sun is not yet at full force.

This brunch has been created especially for the seafood lover. A glass of chilled champagne, along with our *Rocky Pointe Shrimp Cocktail*, is the perfect start to this occasion. One of our most requested recipes, the *Pecan-Crusted Crab Cakes with Chipotle Remoulade*, makes the perfect accompaniment to the *Chorizo, Egg and Potato Tacos* and our summery *Nopalitos, Shrimp, and Cherry Tomato Salad*. A *Tres Leches Cake* garnished with fresh fruit is the ultimate finish for a relaxing morning in the garden.

ROCKY POINTE SHRIMP COCKTAIL

SERVES: 12

Directions:

1. CAREFULLY PRESS A SERRATED KNIFE INTO EACH AVOCADO UNTIL IT MAKES CONTACT WITH THE SEED. HOLDING THE KNIFE AGAINST THE SEED, ROTATE THE FRUIT TO SPLIT IT IN HALF LENGTHWISE.

2. SEPARATE THE TWO HALVES WITH A SLIGHT TWIST, WHICH WILL LEAVE THE WHOLE SEED IMBEDDED IN ONE OF THE HALVES. WITH A SPOON, CAREFULLY SCOOP OUT THE SEED, LEAVING THE FLESH INTACT.

3. HOLD EACH AVOCADO HALF SKIN-SIDE DOWN AND INSERT THE SPOON BETWEEN THE SKIN AND FLESH. RUN THE SPOON AROUND THE ENTIRE FRUIT, SEPARATING THE SKIN FROM THE FLESH. REPEAT WITH REMAINING AVOCADO HALVES.

4. PLACE EACH HALF, FLAT-SIDE DOWN, ON A CUTTING BOARD. CUT IN TWO DIRECTIONS TO CREATE THE DICE.

5. MIX AVOCADOS AND REMAINING INGREDIENTS IN A LARGE MIXING BOWL.

6. CHILL FOR A MINIMUM OF 4 HOURS OR OVERNIGHT.

7. SERVE IN MARTINI GLASSES AND GARNISH WITH FRESH CILANTRO SPRIGS AND LOTS OF FRESH TORTILLA CHIPS FOR DIPPING.

Note: *Selecting a ripe avocado is the most important step. It should be firm, not soft, with the squeeze resistance of a ripe peach or nectarine.*

Ingredients:

4 AVOCADOS, DICED

2 LBS. SMALL SHRIMP, COOKED, PEELED & DEVEINED

2 CUPS GREEN ONIONS, CHOPPED

1/2 CUP JALAPEÑO PEPPERS, CHOPPED

4 CUPS ROMA TOMATOES, DICED

1 LARGE CUCUMBER, PEELED, SEEDED, & FINELY DICED

4 CUPS TOMATO JUICE

1 CUP KETCHUP

1/2 TBSP. FRESH-GROUND BLACK PEPPER

3/4 CUP LIME JUICE

1/2 CUP FRESH CILANTRO, CHOPPED

2 TBSP. SALT (OR TO TASTE)

To Serve
FRESH CILANTRO SPRIGS FOR GARNISH

TORTILLA CHIPS FOR DIPPING

SERVES: 4-6

PECAN-CRUSTED CRAB CAKES WITH CHIPOTLE REMOULADE

Ingredients:

Crab Cakes

1 LB. COOKED CRABMEAT

1 LARGE SWEET POTATO,
    ROASTED 35 MINUTES
    AT 350°

$1/4$ CUP MAYONNAISE

$1/4$ CUP WHIPPING CREAM

1 TBSP. FRESH CILANTRO,
    MINCED

1 PINCH CINNAMON

1 TBSP. DIJON MUSTARD

$1/2$ CUP POBLANO PEPPERS,
    ROASTED, PEELED
    & DICED

$1/2$ CUP FRESH CORN,
    ROASTED

1 TSP. SALT (OR TO TASTE)

Breading

1 CUP PECANS, MEDIUM
    PIECES

$1 1/2$ CUPS JAPANESE
    BREAD CRUMBS
    (PANKO CRUMBS*)

1 CUP EGG WASH
    (1 CUP MILK
    & 2 EGGS)

1 CUP FLOUR

Directions:

Chipotle Remoulade

$1/4$ CUP CHIPOTLE CHILES,
    IN ADOBO SAUCE

2 CUPS MAYONNAISE

2 TBSP. PICKLE RELISH

2 TBSP. CELERY, FINELY DICED

1 TBSP. ONION, FINELY DICED

2 TBSP. KETCHUP

1 TBSP. WORCESTERSHIRE SAUCE

1 TBSP. FRESH GARLIC, MINCED

1. IN BLENDER, PUREE CHIPOTLES WITH MAYONNAISE. SCRAPE
   INTO A BOWL AND WHISK IN REMAINING INGREDIENTS. CHILL.

Crab Cakes

1. IF USING FROZEN CRAB, THAW AND SQUEEZE DRY. RESERVE
   JUICE. PICK THROUGH CRAB FOR SHELL AND CARTILAGE.

2. PEEL SWEET POTATO AND COARSELY MASH IN BOWL. ADD
   MAYONNAISE, CREAM, CILANTRO, CINNAMON AND MUSTARD.
   STIR TO MIX WELL. ADD CRABMEAT, PEPPERS, ROASTED
   CORN AND SALT. IF MIX SEEMS TOO DRY, ADD A LITTLE
   RESERVED CRAB JUICE UNTIL MOISTENED AND SCOOPABLE.

3. PLACE PECANS AND JAPANESE BREAD CRUMBS IN A FOOD
   PROCESSOR AND PULSE TO COMBINE AND PRODUCE A
   MEDIUM SIZE MEAL FOR BREADING.

4. SCOOP OUT DESIRED SIZE OF CRAB MIXTURE AND PAT INTO
   CAKES ABOUT $1/2$" THICK.

5. SET UP A BREADING AREA WITH CRAB CAKES, FLOUR,
   EGG-WASH, AND PECAN-CRUMBS. BREAD THE CAKES BY
   DIPPING INTO FLOUR, THEN EGG-WASH, AND THEN THE
   PECAN-CRUMBS. CHILL WELL, AT LEAST 2 HOURS.

To Serve:

DEEP FRY OR PAN-FRY UNTIL HOT AND CRISPY
GOLDEN BROWN. SERVE WITH THE CHILE REMOULADE AND A
FRESH LEMON WEDGE. MAKES A GREAT APPETIZER OR ENTRÉE
WITH SOME FIESTA SLAW (PAGE 10).

Unseasoned coarse bread crumbs can be substituted for Panko.

CHORIZO, EGG & POTATO TACOS WITH SALSA FRESCA

SERVES: 6

Directions:

Salsa Fresca (YIELD: 6-8 CUPS)

1. PURÉE ALL INGREDIENTS, IN BATCHES, IN A BLENDER OR FOOD PROCESSOR. SALSA SHOULD BE A LITTLE CHUNKY.
2. LET REST 15 MINUTES THEN ADJUST SALT LEVEL IF NECESSARY.
3. CHILL AND ENJOY ON EVERYTHING!

Tacos

1. PREHEAT OVEN TO 400°.
2. HEAT TORTILLAS IN OVEN FOR 2 MINUTES.
3. IN A NON-STICK SKILLET, COMBINE CHORIZO AND POTATOES. HEAT THROUGH.
4. WHEN HOT, POUR IN WHIPPED EGGS.
5. STIR UNTIL BARELY SET AND FLUFFY.
6. FILL HOT TORTILLAS WITH MIXTURE AND TOP WITH SOME SHREDDED CHEESE.
7. PLACE ON LARGE SERVING PLATTER.
8. SERVE WITH A BOWL OF SALSA FRESCA.

NEW MEXICAN RED CHILES

Long, ripe red Anaheim-type chiles, grown mainly around Hatch, New Mexico where they develop their medium heat. Sun dried and sold in whole pods or ground form—known as "New Mexican Red Chile Powder."

Ingredients:

Salsa Fresca

6 ROMA TOMATOES, DICED

2 CANS (14 OZ.) DICED TOMATOES, IN JUICE

2 LARGE RED BELL PEPPERS, SEEDED & DICED

2 LARGE GREEN BELL PEPPERS, SEEDED & DICED

2 ONIONS, DICED

6-8 JALAPEÑOS, STEMMED

1 BUNCH CILANTRO, ROUGHLY CHOPPED

2 TBSP. DRIED OREGANO

1 TBSP. GROUND CUMIN

1 TBSP. SALT

1/4 CUP NEW MEXICAN RED CHILE POWDER

3/4 CUP RED WINE VINEGAR

1/2 CUP TABASCO® PEPPER SAUCE

Tacos

12 (6") FLOUR TORTILLAS, WARMED

2 CUPS MEXICAN CHORIZO, COOKED & DRAINED

2 CUPS POTATOES, BOILED & DICED

12 EGGS, WHIPPED

2 CUPS MIXED JACK & CHEDDAR CHEESE, SHREDDED

1 CUP SALSA FRESCA

SERVES: 12

NOPALITOS, SHRIMP & CHERRY TOMATO SALAD WITH CHILE-LIME VINAIGRETTE

Ingredients:

Salad

3 BAGS (5 OZ.) MIXED
SALAD GREENS

2 JARS (16 OZ.) PICKLED
NOPALITOS, DRAINED
& RINSED

2 PTS. CHERRY TOMATOES,
CUT IN HALF

2 LBS. MEDIUM SHRIMP,
DEVEINED, PEELED
COOKED & CHILLED

2 CUPS CORN, BLANCHED
AND CUT FROM COB

1 CUP COOKED BLACK
BEANS, RINSED

2 MEDIUM RED ONIONS,
SLICED INTO
THIN RINGS

1/2 CUP STUFFED GREEN
OLIVES, SLICED

1 RECIPE CHILE-LIME
VINAIGRETTE

Directions:

Chile-Lime Vinaigrette (YIELDS: 1 1/2 CUPS)

1 CUP OLIVE OIL

1/4 CUP BALSAMIC VINEGAR

2 TBSP. DIJON MUSTARD

1 TBSP. FRESH GARLIC, MINCED

1 TBSP. FRESH-SQUEEZED LIME JUICE

1 TBSP. RED CHILE POWDER

1/2 TSP. RED CHILE FLAKES

1 TSP. SUGAR

1 TSP. SALT

1 TSP. FRESH-GROUND BLACK PEPPER

1/4 CUP FRESH, RINSED AND CHOPPED CILANTRO

1/4 CUP FRESH, RINSED AND CHOPPED BASIL

2 TBSP. FRESH, RINSED AND CHOPPED GREEN ONIONS

1. WHISK TOGETHER ALL INGREDIENTS EXCEPT HERBS
   AND ONIONS.
2. WHEN SUGAR AND SALT ARE DISSOLVED, STIR IN HERBS
   AND GREEN ONIONS.
3. LET FLAVORS BLEND AT LEAST 30 MINUTES BEFORE USING.

Salad

1. ARRANGE GREENS ON PLATTER.
2. SCATTER NOPALITOS OVER GREENS.
3. MAKE AN OUTSIDE RING OF THE CHERRY TOMATOES, THEN
   SHRIMP, THEN CORN, THEN BLACK BEANS.
4. SCATTER ONION RINGS OVER THESE CIRCLES AND THEN
   SPRINKLE WITH OLIVE SLICES AND CHILL.
5. WHEN READY TO SERVE, DRIZZLE ON THE CHILE-LIME
   VINAIGRETTE.

TRES LECHES CAKE WITH MARINATED FRUIT

SERVES: 6-8

Directions:

1. PREHEAT OVEN TO 325°.

2. WITH ELECTRIC MIXER, BEAT EGG WHITES UNTIL SOFT PEAKS FORM.

3. IN ANOTHER BOWL, BEAT EGG YOLKS WITH SUGAR UNTIL LIGHT AND LEMONY COLORED.

4. ADD OIL TO YOLK MIXTURE AND THEN SPRINKLE ON FLOUR. MIX TO INCORPORATE.

5. LIGHTEN THIS BATTER WITH A SCOOP OF EGG WHITES. THEN FOLD REMAINING EGG WHITES INTO THIS MIXTURE. TAKE CARE NOT TO DEFLATE THE BATTER.

6. BUTTER A 9" X 9" GLASS BAKING PAN. ADD BATTER TO THE PAN.

7. BAKE IN 325° OVEN FOR 20-25 MINUTES UNTIL PUFFED AND LIGHT GOLDEN.

8. REMOVE FROM OVEN AND COOL ON A RACK 1 HOUR.

9. MIX THE THREE MILKS WITH RUM.

10. PUNCH HOLES ALL OVER THE CAKE WITH TINES OF A FORK.

11. POUR MILK OVER CAKE. REFRIGERATE FOR A MINIMUM OF 4 HOURS OR OVERNIGHT TO ALLOW CAKE TO SATURATE WITH MILKS.

12. SLICE BERRIES OR CRUSH SLIGHTLY. SLICE THE STONE FRUITS AND MIX LIGHTLY WITH BERRIES. DRIZZLE WITH ORANGE-BRANDY LIQUEUR AND CHILL 30 MINUTES BEFORE SERVING.

13. SCOOP SERVINGS OF CAKE WITH MILK SAUCE INTO SERVING GOBLETS OR BOWLS AND TOP WITH A LITTLE OF THE MARINATED FRUIT.

* Fruits with stones (pits) such as peaches, plums, nectarines, apricots, etc.

Ingredients:

6 LARGE EGGS, SEPARATED

1 CUP SUGAR

1/2 CUP VEGETABLE OIL

1 CUP FLOUR

1 CUP CONDENSED MILK

1 CUP WHOLE MILK

1 CUP EVAPORATED MILK

1/2 CUP SPICED RUM

Topping

1 CUP FRESH BERRIES

2 PCS. STONE FRUIT*

1 OZ. ORANGE-BRANDY LIQUEUR

Star Gazing Party

Guacamole Tostadas
with Pico de Gallo

Spiced Chicken &
Carnitas Taco Bar

Santa Fe Rice Pilaf

Boracho Beans

Summer Fruit Salad

Mexican Hot Chocolate

The air in the Southwest mountains has a clear, dry quality unlike any in the world. When you get away from the city lights, the stars are so close and plentiful it seems as if you could reach up and touch them. In July and August, the Perseid Meteor showers fill the night skies with a display of shooting stars that rivals Independence Day's fireworks.

This meal is the perfect prelude to this astral event and is intended for a large group of fellow astronomers. Create a lavish buffet table with *Guacamole Tostadas with Pico de Gallo, Spiced Chicken and Carnitas Tacos, Santa Fe Rice Pilaf, Boracho Beans* and a fresh *Summer Fruit Salad*.

Complete this experience with some wonderfully colorful blankets, a thermos of the *Mexican Hot Chocolate* and your own special spot under the starry sky.

GUACAMOLE TOSTADAS WITH PICO DE GALLO

SERVES: 12

Directions:

Guacamole
1. COMBINE THE GUACAMOLE INGREDIENTS.
2. MASH WITH A WIRE WHISK UNTIL LUMPY-SMOOTH.

Pico de Gallo
1. TOSS TOGETHER THE INGREDIENTS FOR PICO DE GALLO AND REFRIGERATE.

Tostadas
1. SPREAD GUACAMOLE EVENLY OVER TORTILLAS AND TOP WITH SHREDDED LETTUCE.
2. GARNISH WITH PICO DE GALLO IN THE CENTER OF EACH AND SERVE THE REMAINING AMOUNT ON THE SIDE.

JALAPEÑOS

The "work horse" of green chiles. Medium to hot in spice. Waxy, dark green, with a fresh flavor that is distinctly jalapeño. Remove seeds and veins to reduce some of the heat.

Ingredients:

Guacamole
4 AVOCADOS, SKINNED & SEEDED
2 TBSP. FRESH CILANTRO, CHOPPED
1/4 CUP RED ONIONS, 1/4" DICE
1 RED BELL PEPPER, ROASTED, PEELED, SEEDED & 1/4" DICE
4 OZ. GOAT CHEESE, CRUMBLED
2 TSP. FRESH GARLIC, MINCED
2 JALAPEÑOS, 1/4" DICE
1/2 TSP. SALT

Pico de Gallo
2 LBS. ROMA TOMATOES, CORED & 1/4" DICE
1 SMALL ONION, 1/4" DICE
2 TBSP. FRESH CILANTRO, CHOPPED
2 JALAPEÑOS, MINCED
1 TSP. FRESH GARLIC, MINCED
4 TSP. FRESH-SQUEEZED LIME JUICE
1 1/2 TSP. SALT

Tostadas
12 CORN TORTILLAS, FRIED CRISP
1 HEAD ICEBERG LETTUCE, SHREDDED

49

SERVES: 12

Ingredients:

Spiced Chicken
2 WHOLE CHICKENS
2 YELLOW ONIONS, CHOPPED
2 GALLONS WATER (ENOUGH TO COVER)

4 TBSP. OLIVE OIL
2 CUPS YELLOW ONIONS, JULIENNED
2 CUPS (ANY COLOR) BELL PEPPERS, JULIENNED
1/2 BUNCH FRESH CILANTRO, STEMMED & CHOPPED
2-3 FRESH JALAPEÑO PEPPERS, CHOPPED
1/2 BUNCH GREEN ONIONS, CHOPPED
4 LARGE FRESH TOMATOES, DICED
1 TBSP. FRESH-GROUND BLACK PEPPER
2 TBSP. GROUND CUMIN
2 TBSP. FRESH GARLIC, MINCED
1-2 TBSP. SALT
1 TBSP. DRIED OREGANO

SANTA FE RICE PILAF

Directions:

Spiced Chicken
1. PLACE CHICKENS AND ONIONS IN A POT. ADD ENOUGH WATER TO COVER.

2. BRING TO A BOIL, REDUCE HEAT AND SIMMER FOR 45-60 MINUTES, OR UNTIL CHICKENS ARE FULLY COOKED AND TENDER.

3. REMOVE CHICKENS AND ALLOW TO COOL. SAVE STOCK FOR OTHER USE.

4. WHEN COOL ENOUGH TO HANDLE, DISCARD SKIN AND CAREFULLY PULL THE MEAT FROM THE BONES.

5. DISCARD BONES AND SHRED MEAT.

6. HEAT OLIVE OIL AND SAUTÉ REMAINING VEGETABLES AND SEASONINGS IN A LARGE PAN UNTIL THEY BEGIN TO SOFTEN (ABOUT 10 MINUTES).

7. ADD CHICKEN. IF MIXTURE SEEMS DRY, ADD A LITTLE WATER. SIMMER UNTIL FLAVORS BLEND. TASTE AND ADD ADDITIONAL SALT IF NECESSARY.

SPICED CHICKEN & CARNITAS TACO BAR (CONT.)

SERVES: 12

Directions:

Carnitas

1. PREHEAT OVEN TO 300°.

2. RUB TENDERLOINS WITH OLIVE OIL UNTIL COATED.

3. COMBINE ALL SPICES AND SEASON TENDERLOINS THOROUGHLY.

4. MARK TENDERLOINS ON GRILL; FINISH ROASTING IN 300° OVEN FOR 10-12 MINUTES.

5. LET REST 10 MINUTES THEN THINLY SLICE MEAT ACROSS THE GRAIN.

6. HEAT MILK, ORANGE JUICE AND LARD OR OIL IN A LARGE NON-STICK SKILLET. ADD CUMIN AND SALT.

7. ADD SLICED TENDERLOIN AND COOK OVER HIGH HEAT UNTIL PORK ABSORBS ALL OF LIQUID AND BEGINS TO "FRY" AND GET CRISPY ON EDGES.

8. WHEN CARAMELIZED NICELY AND A LITTLE CRISPY, YOUR "QUICK" CARNITAS ARE READY.

9. MIX ONION AND CILANTRO.

To Serve:

CREATE THE TACO BAR WITH SERVING DISHES FILLED WITH THE SPICED CHICKEN AND CARNITAS. SERVE HOT, WITH PLENTY OF WARM CORN AND FLOUR TORTILLAS AND YOUR FAVORITE GARNISHES AND SALSAS. ACCOMPANY THE TACO BAR WITH SANTA FE RICE PILAF (PAGE 52) AND BORACHO BEANS (PAGE 53).

Ingredients:

Carnitas

3 LBS. PORK TENDERLOINS (ABOUT 2 TRIMMED)

1 TBSP. OLIVE OIL

1 TBSP. NEW MEXICAN RED CHILE POWDER

1 TBSP. KOSHER SALT

1 TBSP. FRESH-GROUND BLACK PEPPER

2 CUPS MILK

1 CUP ORANGE JUICE

3 TBSP. LARD OR VEGETABLE OIL

1/2 TSP. GROUND CUMIN

1 TSP. SALT (OR TO TASTE)

Garnishes

1 CUP WHITE ONION, MINCED

1/2 CUP FRESH CILANTRO, CHOPPED

CORN AND FLOUR TORTILLAS, WARMED

1/4 HEAD GREEN CABBAGE, FINELY SHREDDED

2 CUPS SALSA (YOUR FAVORITE)

SERVES: 12

SANTA FE RICE PILAF

Ingredients:

3 TBSP. BUTTER

1/2 CUP ZUCCHINI,
   FINELY DICED

1/2 CUP RED ONION, DICED

1/2 CUP RED BELL
   PEPPERS, DICED

1/2 CUP GREEN BELL
   PEPPERS, DICED

1/2 CUP POBLANO
   PEPPERS, DICED

1 TSP. NEW MEXICAN
   RED CHILE POWDER

1 TSP. GROUND CUMIN

1 TBSP. FRESH CILANTRO,
   CHOPPED

1/2 CUP CORN, ROASTED

1 CUP BLACK-EYED PEAS,
   COOKED, DRAINED
   & RINSED

1/2 CUP WATER

6 CUPS WHITE RICE,
   COOKED & COOLED

1 TSP. SALT (OR TO TASTE)

1 TSP. FRESH-GROUND
   BLACK PEPPER
   (OR TO TASTE)

1 BUNCH FRESH SPINACH,
   WASHED, STEMMED
   & SLICED

Directions:

1. MELT BUTTER OVER MEDIUM-HIGH HEAT AND SAUTÉ ZUCCHINI, ONION AND PEPPERS FOR ABOUT 3-4 MINUTES.

2. ADD REMAINING INGREDIENTS EXCEPT SPINACH.

3. COOK UNTIL HEATED THOROUGHLY THEN SEASON WITH SALT AND PEPPER TO TASTE.

4. TOSS SLICED SPINACH INTO HOT RICE TO WILT AND SERVE.

Boracho Beans

Directions:

1. Rinse all beans in a colander and place in a 4 qt. pot.
2. Add all remaining ingredients.
3. Add just enough water to cover the beans.
4. Simmer over medium heat 20-30 minutes or until flavors blend and bean juice has slightly thickened.

Ingredients:

4 cups black beans (canned or cooked)

4 cups pinto beans (canned or cooked)

4 cups red beans (canned or cooked)

2 bottles (12 oz.) Mexican beer

1 cup yellow onion, medium dice

1 cup red bell pepper, medium dice

1 cup tomato, medium dice

3 green onions, thinly sliced

3 tbsp fresh cilantro, chopped

1 tbsp. fresh garlic, minced

2 jalapeños, minced (or more to taste)

1 tbsp. fresh-ground black pepper

2 tsp. salt

1 tsp ground cumin

2 qts. water (or more as needed)

SERVES: 6

SUMMER FRUIT SALAD

Ingredients:

2 OZ. ORANGE-BRANDY
   LIQUEUR (OR APPLE
   JUICE)

$1/4$ CUP SUGAR

$1/4$ CUP MINT, CUT IN
   THIN SHREDS

1 STAR FRUIT, CUT
   INTO $1/4"$ SLICES

1 PEELED KIWI, CUT
   INTO $1/4"$ SLICES

$1/2$ PINT RASPBERRIES

$1/2$ PINT BLACKBERRIES

$1/2$ PINT BLUEBERRIES

$1/2$ PINT STRAWBERRIES,
   STEMMED & HALVED

1 BANANA, PEELED &
   CUT INTO $1"$ SLICES

1 BUNCH GREEN OR RED
   GRAPES, WASHED
   & STEMMED
   (ABOUT 2 CUPS)

Directions:

1. IN A LARGE BOWL, MIX ORANGE-BRANDY LIQUEUR (OR APPLE JUICE) WITH SUGAR AND MINT UNTIL SUGAR DISSOLVES.

2. GENTLY ADD FRUITS AND TOSS TO DISTRIBUTE DRESSING. TOSS CAREFULLY SO AS NOT TO BRUISE OR CRUSH FRUIT.

3. COVER AND REFRIGERATE FOR AT LEAST 30 MINUTES.

4. SERVE IN A CHILLED SHALLOW BOWL WITH WHIPPED CREAM IF DESIRED.

Note: For individual servings, this looks great in brightly colored margarita or martini glasses, garnished with a crisp cookie like a biscochito (Page 61) or biscotti.

MEXICAN HOT CHOCOLATE

SERVES: 6

Directions:

1. HEAT MILK TO A SIMMER. DO NOT ALLOW TO BOIL.
2. CHOP CHOCOLATE AND ADD TO PAN.
3. WHISK UNTIL MELTED.
4. ADD VANILLA AND CINNAMON.
5. HEAT UNTIL VERY HOT AND WHISK UNTIL FROTHY.
6. SERVE IN TALL MUGS TOPPED WITH WHIPPED CREAM, IF DESIRED, AND SPRINKLE WITH CINNAMON OR CHOCOLATE.

Ingredients:

2 QTS. MILK

1 LB. MEXICAN CHOCOLATE ᶜ

1 TBSP. VANILLA EXTRACT

1 TBSP. GROUND MEXICAN CINNAMON OR 4 CANELA STICKS ᶜ

MEXICAN CHOCOLATE

A hard, sugary chocolate made with *Canela.*ᶜ It is usually sold in large-size tablets that can be dissolved in hot milk or grated into cake batters or onto bakery items. If unavailable, bittersweet chocolate and cinnamon can be substituted.

Poblano Chicken Chowder

White Cheese Quesadillas
with Warm Peach Salsa

Heirloom Tomato Salad
with Goat Cheese

Green Chile Pesto Chicken Pasta Salad

Biscochitos

Late Summer Rain

In parts of the Southwest, the late Summer heat can linger for so long that it seems as if one more moment will be intolerable. Then suddenly, storm clouds build on the horizon, the sun disappears and the rumble of thunder rolls across the sky. These fast and furious storms break the heat and leave a cooling peace behind them—usually after they have ruined all plans for cooking dinner outdoors.

After the rain passes, dry your patio furniture, grab a light sweater and a glass of wine and enjoy this tasty summer meal. Serve the *Poblano Chicken Chowder* first and then follow with our *White Cheese Quesadillas with Warm Peach Salsa* and two summery salads—*Heirloom Tomato with Goat Cheese*, and *Green Chile Pesto Chicken Pasta*. The crispy *Biscochitos* are perfect for dipping in a last cup of coffee.

POBLANO CHICKEN CHOWDER

SERVES: 6-8

Directions:

1. MAKE A ROUX BY HEATING MELTED BUTTER WITH FLOUR AND WHISKING OVER MEDIUM-HIGH HEAT FOR 5 MINUTES. DO NOT BROWN THIS MIXTURE. IT SHOULD BE A BLOND COLOR. RESERVE.

2. HEAT OIL IN A LARGE KETTLE, ADD ONIONS, CELERY, CARROTS, POBLANOS AND GARLIC. SAUTÉ UNTIL ONIONS BECOME TRANSLUCENT AND CARROTS BEGIN TO SOFTEN.

3. ADD THYME, PEPPER AND CUMIN STIR WELL. ADD CHICKEN STOCK.

4. BRING TO A BOIL, REDUCE TO SIMMER AND COOK 20 MINUTES OR UNTIL VEGETABLES ARE SOFT.

5. BEGIN ADDING ROUX AND WHISK IN EACH BIT TO INCORPORATE. BE CAREFUL NOT TO FORM LUMPS!

6. CONTINUE TO COOK OVER HIGH HEAT FOR 5 MINUTES TO REMOVE THE FLOUR TASTE.

7. REMOVE FROM HEAT AND ADD TABASCO® SAUCE AND CILANTRO.

8. ADD CREAM AND DICED CHICKEN. HEAT THROUGH.

9. TOP WITH CRISP TORTILLA STRIPS AND JACK CHEESE, IF DESIRED.

Ingredients:

Roux
1 STICK UNSALTED BUTTER, MELTED
3/4 CUP FLOUR

Soup Base
1 TBSP. OLIVE OIL
1/2 LB. ONION, DICED
1/2 LB. CELERY, DICED
1/2 LB. CARROTS, DICED
1/4 LB. POBLANO CHILES, SEEDED & DICED
1 TBSP. FRESH GARLIC, MINCED
1 TSP. THYME LEAVES
1/2 TBSP. WHITE PEPPER
1 TBSP. GROUND CUMIN
2 QTS. STRONG CHICKEN STOCK (OR CHICKEN BOUILLON/WATER)
1 1/2 TBSP. TABASCO® PEPPER SAUCE
1/2 BUNCH CILANTRO, WASHED & FINELY CHOPPED

To Serve Soup
1 QT. HEAVY CREAM
1 LB. CHICKEN BREAST, GRILLED & DICED
JACK CHEESE, SHREDDED (OPTIONAL)

POBLANO PEPPERS

Fresh, large, dark green chile peppers with rounded shoulder tapering to tip. Medium to spicy hot. Great peeled, seeded and stuffed for chili rellenos. When dry they are called *Ancho Chilies*, a must for making *Moles*.

57

Serves: 6

White Cheese Quesadillas with Warm Peach Salsa

Ingredients:

Warm Peach Salsa

3 TBSP. BUTTER

2 CUPS FRESH PEACHES, DICED

2 TBSP. GREEN ONIONS, CHOPPED

$1/4$ CUP RED BELL PEPPER, FINELY DICED

2-3 TBSP. GRAPEFRUIT JUICE

1 TBSP. BROWN SUGAR

1 TSP. RED PEPPER FLAKES

4 TSP. FRESH CILANTRO, CHOPPED,

1 PINCH SALT (OR TO TASTE)

Quesadillas

6 (10-12") WHEAT TORTILLAS

4 TBSP. BUTTER, MELTED

4 CUPS QUESO FRESCO, CRUMBLED

$1/2$ CUP COTIJA CHEESE, CRUMBLED

1 RECIPE WARM PEACH SALSA

Directions:

Warm Peach Salsa (Yield: 2 $1/2$ cups)

1. Melt butter. Add peaches, green onions and bell peppers.

2. Saute 2-3 minutes until just warm.

3. Add juice, sugar, pepper flakes and cilantro. Heat to melt sugar.

4. Remove from heat and add salt if necessary.

5. Serve warm with white cheese quesadillas (below). Also great with grilled chicken or pork tenderloin.

Quesadillas

1. Preheat a griddle or non-stick skillet to medium-hot.

2. Place tortillas on a sheet pan and brush one side with butter.

3. Turn over and place $3/4$ cup queso fresco cheese and a sprinkling of cotija on one half of the tortilla. Fold in half, buttered side out.

4. On the pre-heated skillet, cook quesadillas until browned and cheese is melted, about 2-3 minutes on each side.

5. Cut each into 4 pieces and serve topped with warm peach salsa.

HEIRLOOM TOMATO SALAD WITH GOAT CHEESE

SERVES: 6

Directions:

Balsamic Vinaigrette

1. WHISK VINEGAR AND SPICES TOGETHER TO DISSOLVE SALT.

2. SLOWLY WHISK IN OIL UNTIL EMULSIFIED.

3. KEEP AT ROOM TEMPERATURE UNTIL READY TO SERVE.

Salad

1. LINE PLATTER WITH OUTTER ROMAINE LEAVES. THINLY SLICE THE REST OF THE LETTUCE HEAD. SCATTER ON A PLATTER.

2. SHINGLE TOMATOES AND GOAT CHEESE ROUNDS ON PLATTER.

3. DRIZZLE WITH BALSAMIC VINAIGRETTE AND SCATTER SEEDS OVER THE TOP.

4. GARNISH WITH SPRIGS OF FRESH OREGANO.

   * Heirloom varieties are available at specialty shops or from your own gardens. Any ripe tomato combination can be used.

Ingredients:

Balsamic Vinaigrette

3/4 CUP BALSAMIC VINEGAR

2 TBSP. FRESH OREGANO, MINCED

1 TBSP. FRESH GARLIC, MINCED

1/2 TSP. SALT

1 TSP. FRESH-GROUND BLACK PEPPER

1 CUP OLIVE OIL

Salad

1 HEAD ROMAINE LETTUCE, CLEANED

2 LBS. HEIRLOOM TOMATOES, CUT INTO 1/2" SLICES

2 (8 OZ.) LOGS GOAT CHEESE, CUT INTO 12 EVEN SLICES

1/2 CUP SUNFLOWER SEEDS, ROASTED & SALTED

FRESH OREGANO SPRIGS FOR GARNISH

SERVES: 6

Ingredients

Salad

1 HEAD ROMAINE LETTUCE, WASHED & SEPARATED

1 RECIPE GREEN CHILE PESTO (SEE RIGHT)

1 LB. COOKED PASTA (ORZO, ELBOW OR PENNE ARE GOOD)

1 LB. SKINLESS & BONELESS GRILLED CHICKEN, DICED OR SHREDDED

2 EARS CORN, ROASTED AND CUT FROM COB

2 LARGE CARROTS, JULIENNED

2 LARGE ZUCCHINI, JULIENNED (GREEN PARTS ONLY)

1 CUP RED ONION, JULIENNED

8 ROMA TOMATOES, QUARTERED

GREEN CHILE PESTO CHICKEN PASTA SALAD

Directions:

Green Chile Pesto (YIELD: 2-3 CUPS)

2 CUPS FRESH OR CANNED, ROASTED GREEN CHILES

1 1/2 CUPS GRATED PARMESAN CHEESE

4 LARGE, FRESH CLOVES GARLIC

3/4 CUP TOASTED PINE NUTS

2 TSP. SALT

1/2 CUP RICE VINEGAR

1/2 TSP. SALT

1 TBSP. FRESH-GROUND BLACK PEPPER

2 CUPS OLIVE OIL

1. PLACE ALL INGREDIENTS, EXCEPT OIL, IN A FOOD PROCESSOR AND PROCESS UNTIL FINELY MINCED.
2. WITH MOTOR RUNNING, SLOWLY BEGIN POURING IN THE OIL UNTIL PESTO IS CREAMY AND SMOOTH.

Other Uses:
1. Mix with softened butter and use to melt over grilled fish, chicken or steak.
2. Toss with a little mayonnaise and cooked, shredded chicken. Use on a sandwich or in a wrap.

Salad
1. LINE A PLATTER WITH THE ROMAINE LEAVES IN A SPOKE PATTERN. CUT HEART OF ROMAINE INTO SMALL STRIPS AND PILE ON LEAVES.
2. IN A LARGE BOWL, TOSS PASTA, CHICKEN, CORN, CARROT AND ZUCCHINI SHREDS AND ONION. TOSS UNTIL EACH PIECE IS WELL COATED WITH PESTO DRESSING.
3. PLACE ON TOP OF THE PREPARED GREENS AND SURROUND WITH QUARTERED TOMATOES.

BISCOCHITOS

Directions:

1. PREHEAT OVEN TO 350°.
2. CREAM TOGETHER BUTTER, SHORTENING, SUGAR AND CRUSHED ANISE SEEDS.
3. SIFT FLOUR WITH SALT AND BAKING POWDER.
4. ADD EGGS AND VANILLA TO CREAMED MIXTURE.
5. ALTERNATELY ADD DRY INGREDIENTS AND ORANGE JUICE TO THE CREAMED MIXTURE.
6. MIX JUST UNTIL ALL INGREDIENTS ARE COMBINED AND DOUGH PULLS AWAY FROM BOWL.
7. REMOVE AND WRAP IN PLASTIC WRAP. REFRIGERATE FOR AT LEAST 30 MINUTES.
8. ROLL OUT $1/4$" THICK AND CUT INTO YOUR FAVORITE SHAPES WITH COOKIE CUTTERS OR A KNIFE.
9. PLACE ON PARCHMENT-LINED COOKIE SHEETS.
10. MIX CINNAMON AND SUGAR.
11. SPRINKLE WITH CINNAMON-SUGAR MIXTURE AND BAKE 6-8 MINUTES, UNTIL EDGES ARE LIGHTLY BROWNED.
12. COOL ON RACK AND STORE IN AIRTIGHT CONTAINERS.

* Traditionally, biscochitos are made with lard, which can be substituted for the butter and shortening in our recipe.

Ingredients:

Biscochitos

1 CUP BUTTER

1 CUP VEGETABLE SHORTENING

1 $1/2$ CUPS SUGAR

1 $1/2$ TSP. ANISE SEEDS, SLIGHTLY CRUSHED

2 LARGE EGGS, SLIGHTLY BEATEN

1 TSP. VANILLA

6 CUPS FLOUR, SIFTED

1 TSP. SALT

1 TBSP. BAKING POWDER

$1/4$ CUP ORANGE JUICE

Topping

1 CUP SUGAR

1 TBSP. GROUND CINNAMON

61

Too Hot to Handle
In the Mountains
Los Días de Los Muertos
Thanksgiving

Autumn

Roasted Fingerling Potatoes with
Orange-Habanero Aioli

Green Chile Chicken Lasagna
with Goat Cheese

Romaine Hearts with
Southwest Caesar Dressing

Chocolate Pecan Pumpkin Squares

Too Hot To Handle

Ah, what would American Southwest cuisine be without chiles?
Corn, beans and squash may be the three staple foods of the
Southwest, but the chile is the quintessential ingredient in this
cuisine. Here, the arrival of Autumn is clearly marked by the
aroma of these flavorful peppers roasting over open flames.

This meal celebrates the chile in all its glory—but don't be
alarmed—chiles don't have to be hot. In their various forms,
chiles can add anything from a simple zest to a flaming inferno.
Serve the *Roasted Fingerling Potatoes with Orange-Habanero Aioli*
as a spicy appetizer. The *Green Chile Chicken Lasagna with Goat
Cheese* and *Romaine Hearts with Southwest Caesar Dressing* are
followed by *Chocolate-Pecan Pumpkin Squares* to complete this
delicious Autumnal feast.

ROASTED FINGERLING POTATOES WITH ORANGE-HABANERO AIOLI

SERVES: 6

Directions:

1. PREHEAT OVEN TO 375°.

2. TOSS POTATOES WITH OLIVE OIL AND HALF THE SALT. PLACE ON A ROASTING PAN AND ROAST AT 375°, STIRRING OCCASIONALLY UNTIL BROWNED AND SLIGHTLY CRISP (ABOUT 10 MINUTES).

3. WHILE ROASTING, MAKE AIOLI.

4. PLACE MAYONNAISE, HABANERO, GARLIC, ZEST AND JUICE IN A BLENDER JAR. PROCESS UNTIL MIXED WELL AND FLAVORS ARE BLENDED. SEASON WITH SALT AND PEPPER IF DESIRED.

5. SERVE POTATOES FAIRLY HOT, SPRINKLED WITH REMAINING KOSHER SALT AND AIOLI ON THE SIDE AS A DIP. BE CAREFUL, DON'T SERVE THESE RIGHT OUT OF THE OVEN TO AVOID BURNING YOUR GUESTS' MOUTHS AND FINGERS.

Ingredients:

Roasted Fingerling Potatoes

1 LB. TINY FINGERLING POTATOES, BOILED JUST UNTIL TENDER

3 TBSP. OLIVE OIL

1 TSP. KOSHER SALT

Orange-Habanero Aioli

1 1/2 CUPS MAYONNAISE

1/2 TSP. HABANERO CHILE, MINCED

2 TBSP. FRESH GARLIC, MINCED

1/2 TSP. ORANGE ZEST

2 TBSP. ORANGE JUICE

SALT & PEPPER TO TASTE

HABANERO CHILES

The smaller they are, the hotter they get! A bright flavored, tropical chile weed found throughout the Yucatan. Very distinct flavor—one of the hottest chiles cultivated today. Use in fruit-based sauces, salsas and marinades. Beware—extremely hot. Use when the 1" chile ripens to an orange-red.

SERVES: 6

GREEN CHILE CHICKEN LASAGNA WITH GOAT CHEESE

Ingredients:

Green Chile Sauce

1 TBSP. OLIVE OIL

1 LARGE YELLOW ONION, PEELED AND DICED

3 LARGE, FRESH CLOVES GARLIC

8 FRESH GREEN CHILES,* ROASTED

3 CUPS CHICKEN STOCK

1/2 CUP CILANTRO

1 TSP. WHOLE MEXICAN OREGANO

1 TSP. GROUND CUMIN

SALT & PEPPER TO TASTE

Lasagna

1 RECIPE GREEN CHILE SAUCE

1 LB. LARGE EGG ROLL SHEETS OR 14 (6") CORN TORTILLAS

8 FRESH GREEN CHILES, ROASTED, PEELED & SEEDED*

1 LOG (6 OZ.) GOAT CHEESE, CRUMBLED

1 LB. JACK CHEESE, SHREDDED (RESERVE 1/3 FOR TOPPING)

1 LB. COOKED CHICKEN, DICED OR SHREDDED

Directions:

Green Chile Sauce (YIELD: 4 CUPS)

1. HEAT OIL IN A LARGE POT AND SAUTÉ ONIONS AND GARLIC OVER MEDIUM HEAT UNTIL TRANSLUCENT.

2. ADD SEEDED GREEN CHILES AND STOCK. BRING TO A SIMMER AND ADD CILANTRO AND SEASONINGS.

3. COOK FOR 3-4 MINUTES THEN CAREFULLY TRANSFER TO BLENDER JAR AND PROCESS UNTIL SMOOTH.

   The sauce will be just as hot as the pepper it is made with. You could use all Poblano for a spicy version, or all Anaheim for a milder version, according to your preference.

Lasagna

1. PREHEAT OVEN TO 350°.

2. SPREAD 1 CUP SAUCE OVER BOTTOM AND UP SIDES OF A 9" X 13" BAKING DISH.

3. MAKE THREE LAYERS IN THE FOLLOWING ORDER:

   1ST LAYER: DOUBLE-LAYERED EGG ROLL SHEETS OR SINGLE-LAYERED TORTILLAS, FLAT CHILES, GOAT CHEESE, 1/3 JACK CHEESE.

   2ND LAYER: DOUBLE-LAYERED EGG ROLL SHEETS OR SINGLE-LAYERED TORTILLAS, 1 CUP SAUCE, CHICKEN, 1/3 JACK CHEESE.

   3RD LAYER: DOUBLE-LAYERED EGG ROLL SHEETS OR SINGLE-LAYERED TORTILLAS, REMAINING SAUCE.

4. COVER WITH PARCHMENT PAPER THEN FOIL. (CAN BE REFRIGERATED FOR UP TO 4 HOURS AT THIS POINT.)

5. BAKE IN PREHEATED OVEN AT 350° FOR ABOUT 40 MINUTES.

6. UNCOVER AND TOP WITH RESERVED JACK CHEESE. RETURN TO OVEN FOR 10 MINUTES TO MELT CHEESE.

7. CUT INTO SERVING-SIZED SQUARES AND SERVE WHILE HOT.

   Canned, whole, roasted and peeled mild green chiles may be substituted.

ROASTING & PEELING PEPPERS

In late summer and early autumn, farmers' markets and roadside stands throughout the Southwest abound with peppers of all kinds and colors. Here they are usually roasted in huge metal drums over open flame, filling the air with their spicy fragrance. If you are not so fortunate as to find freshly roasted peppers, it is quite simple to do at home.

Poblano, anaheim, jalapeño and red and yellow bell peppers are ideal for roasting.

1. Place washed peppers under a broiler or on a very hot grill until the skin blisters and blackens all over. Do this, turning often, and being careful not to cook—you only want to blacken the skin. If you are roasting only one or two peppers, this can also be done by sticking a pepper on a long-handled cooking fork and holding it over the open gas flame of your stove. Again, be certain only to blacken the skin, not to cook the pepper itself.

2. Remove blackened peppers from the heat and quickly place in a plastic bag. Let steam for 2-3 minutes.

3. Remove the skins from the meat of the peppers and discard. Remember to wear gloves if using hotter chile varieties. Once the skin is removed, the peppers can be quickly rinsed under water, but this will take a little flavor away.

4. From this point, if using for chili rellenos, slit the pepper down one side and carefully remove the seeds, leaving the stem intact. You can stuff, chop or purée as desired. Roasted peppers will keep for several days in a plastic bag or container in the refrigerator. Do not keep in metal containers or they will take on a tinny flavor and can damage the container's finish. To keep longer, freeze until ready to use.

SERVES: 6

Ingredients:

Southwest Caesar Dressing

1 CUP DIJON MUSTARD

1 CUP MAYONNAISE

2 TBSP. WORCESTERSHIRE SAUCE

2 TBSP. FRESH CILANTRO

1 TBSP. FRESH-SQUEEZED LEMON JUICE

4 ANCHOVIES

1 TSP. FRESH-GROUND BLACK PEPPER

1 TSP. TABASCO® PEPPER SAUCE

4 TBSP. RED WINE VINEGAR

4 CLOVES GARLIC

1 TSP. SALT

Salad

2 HEADS ROMAINE LETTUCE

2 LARGE TOMATOES, $1/2$" DICE

$1/2$ CUP COTIJA^L CRUMBLES OR PARMESAN SHREDS

2 CUPS FRIED TORTILLA STRIPS

SOUTHWEST CAESAR SALAD

Directions:

Southwest Caesar Dressing

1. PLACE DRESSING INGREDIENTS IN A BLENDER AND BLEND ON HIGH UNTIL SMOOTH.

Salad

1. REMOVE OUTER LEAVES FROM ROMAINE AND CUT INTO QUARTERED WEDGES LENGTHWISE. RINSE UNDER COLD WATER, SHAKE OFF EXCESS WATER, THEN LAY WEDGES ON A PLATE IN THE REFRIGERATOR TO DRAIN UNTIL VERY COLD (ABOUT 30 MINUTES). THIS CRISPENS THE ROMAINE.

2. PLACE EACH WEDGE ON A DECORATIVE PLATE. DRIZZLE THE DRESSING DOWN EACH WEDGE, ALLOWING SOME TO RUN ONTO THE PLATE.

3. SPRINKLE THE LARGE DICED TOMATOES AND COTIJA OR PARMESAN OVER THE LETTUCE AND THE PLATE.

4. MAKE A $1/3$ CUP MOUND OF THE TORTILLA STRIPS ON THE CENTER OF EACH WEDGE.

CHOCOLATE PECAN PUMPKIN SQUARES

SERVES: 6

Directions:

Pie Filling & Crust

1. PREHEAT OVEN TO 350°.
2. COMBINE PIE FILLING INGREDIENTS IN A MIXER WITH PADDLE ATTACHMENT AND MIX WELL.
3. COMBINE MELTED BUTTER WITH GROUND PECANS AND CHOCOLATE CRUMBS.
4. PRESS INTO A 9" X 14" BAKING PAN.
5. TOP WITH THE PIE FILLING, SPREADING EVENLY.
6. BAKE AT 350° FOR 25-30 MINUTES OR UNTIL A KNIFE INSERTED INTO THE CENTER COMES OUT CLEAN, SHOWING THE FILLING IS SET.
7. REMOVE FROM OVEN AND LET COOL. CHILL IF DESIRED OR SERVE AT ROOM TEMPERATURE.

Topping

1. PREPARE TOPPING BY SPLITTING AND SCRAPING SEEDS OF THE VANILLA BEAN INTO A CHILLED BOWL WITH CREAM, HONEY AND SUGAR.
2. WHIP INTO STIFF PEAKS. KEEP CHILLED UNTIL READY TO SERVE.

To Serve:

CUT PIE INTO SQUARES OF DESIRED SIZE, TOP WITH WHIPPED CREAM AND DRIZZLE WITH CHOCOLATE SYRUP.

Ingredients:

Pie Filling

20 OZ. SOLID PACK PUMPKIN, CANNED (OR FRESH, ROASTED & PUREED)

3 LARGE EGGS

3/4 CUP SUGAR

3/4 CUP EVAPORATED MILK

1 1/4 TSP. GROUND CINNAMON

1/2 TSP. SALT

1/4 TSP. GROUND GINGER

Crust

1/2 CUP UNSALTED BUTTER, MELTED

1 3/4 CUPS CHOCOLATE COOKIE CRUMBS

1/2 CUP PECANS, CHOPPED IN PROCESSOR UNTIL FINE

Topping

1 CUP HEAVY CREAM

1" PIECE OF VANILLA BEAN, SPLIT

1 TBSP. HONEY

1 TBSP. SUGAR

CHOCOLATE SYRUP, AS NEEDED FOR GARNISH

Roast Pork Tenderloin Tortas
with Pickled Onions

Chicken Mole Tamales

Apple-Jicama Slaw with
Honey-Chipotle Vinaigrette

Piñon Pralines

Hot Spiced Cider with
Mexican Cinnamon Sticks

In the Mountains

Autumn's beautiful colors and crisp air encourage us to
make the most of the season. The rich colors and textures
of the Southwest inspired this meal, which is ideally suited
for an Autumnal picnic in the Mountains.

Pack a large basket with the *Roast Pork Tenderloin Tortas with
Pickled Onions*, *Chicken Mole Tamales* and our *Apple-Jicama Slaw*.
Don't forget to add the *Piñon Pralines* and a thermos of *Hot
Spiced Cider with Mexican Cinnamon Sticks* for the perfect
finishing touch.

ROAST PORK TENDERLOIN TORTAS WITH PICKLED ONIONS

SERVES: 6

Directions:

1. WHISK TOGETHER MARINADE INGREDIENTS FOR PORK. PLACE IN A ZIPPER-CLOSE PLASTIC BAG AND ADD TENDERLOINS. MARINATE FOR A MINIMUM OF 4 HOURS OR OVER NIGHT.

2. **Pickled Onions**
   - 1 MEDIUM RED ONION, THINLY SLICED
   - 1 CUP WHITE WINE
   - $1/2$ CUP RED WINE VINEGAR
   - 2 TSP. SALT

   PLACE ALL INGREDIENTS IN A SMALL POT AND COOK UNTIL ONIONS ARE SOFT AND THE LIQUID IS ALMOST COMPLETELY REDUCED. CHILL.

3. **Guajillo Salsa**
   - 3 GUAJILLO PEPPERS
   - 1 LARGE TOMATO
   - $1/2$ LARGE ONION, CHOPPED
   - $1/4$ CUP OLIVE OIL
   - 1 TBSP. FRESH GARLIC
   - 2 TSP. BLACK PEPPER
   - 1 CUP WATER

   COMBINE ALL INGREDIENTS AND BRING TO A BOIL. COOK 10 MINUTES THEN COOL. PUREE ALL IN BLENDER. FRY THIS PASTE IN THE OLIVE OIL UNTIL SLIGHTLY THICKENED. CHILL.

4. ROAST THE PORK AT $425°$ FOR 15-20 MINUTES MINUTES. LET REST 5-10 MINUTES BEFORE SLICING.

Tortas

5. TOP BREAD BOTTOMS WITH SLICED PORK. WRAP IN FOIL AND TAKE TO PICNIC.

6. HEAT TORTAS (IN FOIL) ON A GRILL UNTIL HOT.

7. OPEN EACH AND TOP WITH SALSA, AVOCADOS, CABBAGE, LETTUCE, TOMATOES, PICKLED ONIONS AND SOUR CREAM. PRESS ON THE TOP AND SCRUNCH TOGETHER.

   * Telera bread is a wide, round Mexican roll. If you are unable to find these, a large sour dough roll or other sturdy roll can be used.

Ingredients:

Marinade

1 CUP PINEAPPLE JUICE

1 CUP CRANBERRY JUICE

$1/4$ CUP SOY SAUCE

1 TBSP. FRESH GARLIC, MINCED

2 TSP. FRESH-GROUND BLACK PEPPER

3 LBS. PORK TENDERLOIN (SILVER SKIN MUST BE REMOVED)

Tortas

6 TELERA ROLLS,* SPLIT IN HALF

1 RECIPE GUAJILLO SALSA (SEE LEFT)

3 AVOCADOS, SLICED

1 CUP RED CABBAGE, SHREDDED

6 LEAVES GREEN-LEAF LETTUCE

12 SLICES FRESH, RIPE TOMATO

1 RECIPE PICKLED ONIONS (SEE LEFT)

6 TBSP. SOUR CREAM

YIELD: 12 TAMALES

CHICKEN MOLE TAMALES

Ingredients:

Tamale Dough

2 LBS. FRESH MASA
   (OR MASA HARINA
   MIXED 50/50 WITH
   WATER)

1/2 LB. VEGETABLE
   SHORTENING, LARD
   OR BUTTER, SOFTENED

1 1/2 TBSP. BAKING
   POWDER

1 TBSP. SALT

12 CORN HUSKS

Chicken Mole Filling

1 LB. COOKED CHICKEN

4 CUPS PECAN MOLE
   SAUCE*

Directions:

1. IF USING MASA HARINA, MIX WITH WATER AND LET REST 10
   MINUTES. IF DOUGH IS TOO DRY, ADD A LITTLE MORE WATER.

2. PLACE IN MIXING BOWL AND BEAT IN SOFTENED SHORTENING,
   BAKING POWDER AND SALT WITH A WOODEN SPOON OR
   PADDLE ATTACHMENT.

3. KEEP BEATING UNTIL MASA IS VERY LIGHT, ABOUT 10 MINUTES.

4. WASH AND SOFTEN CORN HUSKS IN HOT WATER. PAT DRY
   AND KEEP COVERED WITH A DAMP TOWEL.

5. SIMMER CHICKEN IN 2 CUPS OF PECAN MOLE SAUCE FOR 10
   MINUTES TO ALLOW CHICKEN TO ABSORB FLAVORS.

6. COOL TO ROOM TEMPERATURE.

7. DIVIDE MASA BETWEEN THE 12 CORN HUSKS. SPREAD ON
   EACH HUSK TO A 3" X 5" AREA.

8. DIVIDE CHICKEN MIXTURE DOWN CENTER OF MASA. ROLL
   HUSK LIKE A CIGAR, SEALING MASA OVER FILLING BY PINCHING
   THE ENDS. TUCK HUSK ENDS UNDER, SO THEY OVERLAP IN
   THE CENTER AND TIE THE TAMALE WITH A STRIP OF HUSK.

9. STEAM TAMALES 1 HOUR OVER MEDIUM HEAT. TAMALES WILL
   BE DONE WHEN MASA PULLS EASILY AWAY FROM THE HUSK.

10. SERVE HOT. PASS EXTRA MOLE IN A PITCHER OR GRAVY BOAT
    TO SPOON ON TOP.

* See page 88 for Pecan Mole Sauce recipe.

APPLE-JICAMA SLAW WITH HONEY-CHIPOTLE VINAIGRETTE

SERVES: 6

Directions:

Honey-Chipotle Vinaigrette (YIELDS: 1 QT)

1. PLACE ALL INGREDIENTS EXCEPT OIL IN A BLENDER. BLEND ON HIGH UNTIL ALL INGREDIENTS ARE SMOOTH.

2. WITH BLENDER RUNNING, SLOWLY DRIZZLE IN OIL UNTIL EMULSIFIED. CHILL.

Apple-Jicama Slaw

1. TOSS SLAW INGREDIENTS WITH VINAIGRETTE IN A LARGE BOWL, TAKING CARE NOT TO BREAK APPLES OR JICAMA STICKS.

2. CHILL UNTIL READY TO SERVE TO ALLOW FLAVORS TO BLEND.

Ingredients:

Honey-Chipotle Vinaigrette
3/4 CUP RED WINE VINEGAR

3/4 CUP DIJON MUSTARD

1/2 TSP. EACH DRIED BASIL, OREGANO, THYME, & DILL

1 TSP. SUGAR

1 TSP. FRESH GARLIC, MINCED

1 TSP. FRESH-GROUND BLACK PEPPER

1 TSP. SALT

1/2 CUP HONEY

1/4 CUP CHIPOTLE CHILES, CANNED IN ADOBO SAUCE

3/4 CUP WATER

2 CUPS VEGETABLE OIL

Apple-Jicama Slaw
3 CUPS JICAMA, PEELED & JULIENNED

3 CUPS GRANNY SMITH APPLES, CORED & JULIENNED

1 RED BELL PEPPER, JULIENNED

3 TBSP. FRESH CILANTRO, CHOPPED

1 CUP HONEY-CHIPOTLE VINAIGRETTE

73

YIELD: 48

PIÑON PRALINES

Ingredients:

4 CUPS BROWN SUGAR

4 CUPS HEAVY CREAM

1/4 TSP. SALT

1/4 TSP. GROUND
    CINNAMON

1 TSP. VANILLA EXTRACT

1/2 STICK BUTTER

2 CUPS ROASTED
    PINE NUTS

2 CUPS PECAN HALVES
    OR PIECES

Directions:

1. MIX SUGAR, CREAM, SALT, CINNAMON AND VANILLA. BRING TO A BOIL OVER HIGH HEAT AND COOK UNCOVERED FOR ABOUT 15 MINUTES. CHECK WITH A CANDY THERMOMETER (260°) OR PUT A DROP INTO SOME ICE WATER. IF IT FORMS A HARD, CHEWY BALL, IT'S READY.

2. TURN OFF HEAT AND ADD BUTTER. QUICKLY STIR IN NUTS AND STIR TO COAT ALL PIECES.

3. WITH A TEASPOON, DROP ONTO PARCHMENT-LINED PANS OR BUTTERED FOIL.

4. LET COOL AT ROOM TEMPERATURE.

5. TRANSFER TO AN AIR TIGHT CONTAINER OR PRETTY COOKIE TIN TO TAKE ON YOUR PICNIC. THESE PRALINES ALSO MAKE A GREAT GIFT WRAPPED IN CELLOPHANE AND TIED WITH RAFFIA.

HOT SPICED CIDER WITH MEXICAN CINNAMON STICKS

SERVES: 8
(8 OZ. PORTIONS)

Directions:

1. PLACE ALL INGREDIENTS IN A SAUCE PAN AND PLACE ON STOVE OVER MEDIUM-HIGH HEAT UNTIL IT COMES TO A BOIL.

2. REDUCE HEAT TO LOW AND SIMMER FOR 10-15 MINUTES.

3. LET STEEP (REST) FOR 20-30 MINUTES.

4. STRAIN CIDER THROUGH A FINE STRAINER. REMOVE THE CANELA STICKS.

5. TO TRANSPORT TO YOUR PICNIC, POUR CIDER INTO A THERMOS.

6. TO SERVE: POUR CIDER INTO TALL MUGS AND GARNISH WITH SLICED APPLES AND CANELA STICKS.

Ingredients:

8 CUPS APPLE CIDER (USE FRESH WHEN AVAILABLE)

1 1/2 TSP. WHOLE ALLSPICE, SLIGHTLY CRACKED

1 TSP. WHOLE CLOVES

1 TSP. WHOLE CORIANDER SEED

1/2 TSP. WHOLE FENNEL SEED

3/4 TSP. GROUND NUTMEG

1/2 TSP. WHOLE CUMIN SEED

6 CANELA STICKS (USE CINNAMON STICKS IF NOT AVAILABLE)

Garnish

2 SMALL, SEEDED AND THINLY SLICED RIPE APPLES

6 CANELA STICKS (USE CINNAMON STICKS IF NOT AVAILABLE)

CANELA STICKS

Mexican cinnamon, "Canela" can be found in ethnic or gourmet sections of grocery stores and smells like Red Hot candies. If unavailable, regular cinnamon can be substituted.

Chicken Chile Rellenos with
Tomatillo-Avocado Salsa

Venison Posole

Noche Buena Salad

Fire-Grilled Turkey Skewers with
Papaya-Mango Salsa &
Cucumber-Mint Dipping Sauce

Braised Buffalo Short Ribs
in Mustard Mole Sauce

Mini Buñuelo Sundae Bar

Los Días de Los Muertos

Contrary to the seemingly gruesome name, The Days of
the Dead are really a joyful celebration of the entire life
cycle. This festival traces its origins to the ancient Aztecs
who believed that death was not an ending but rather a
stepping stone from one stage of existence to another. As
the indigenous peoples of the Southwest were converted
to Christianity, pre-Hispanic rituals blended with All Saints'
Day on November 1st and All Souls' Day on November 2nd.
Many special foods are traditionally served at this time
including breads, candies, meats and especially chocolate.

Create your own autumnal party with *Chicken Chile Rellenos
with Tomatillo-Avocado Salsa, Venison Posole, Noche Buena Salad,
Fire-Grilled Turkey Skewers* garnished with *Papaya-Mango Salsa*
and *Cucumber Mint Dipping Sauce* and *Braised Buffalo Short
Ribs in Mustard Mole.* Finish the evening with a *Mini Buñuelo
Sundae Bar.*

CHICKEN CHILE RELLENOS WITH TOMATILLO-AVOCADO SALSA

SERVES: 12

Directions:

Tomatillo-Avocado Salsa (YIELD: ABOUT 3 CUPS)
1. PLACE TOMATILLOS AND WATER IN A SAUCEPAN AND BRING TO BOIL. REDUCE HEAT AND SIMMER FOR 5 MINUTES. DRAIN, RESERVING LIQUID.
2. PLACE TOMATILLOS, AVOCADO FLESH, JALAPENO, GREEN ONIONS, CILANTRO, SOUR CREAM AND SALT IN A BLENDER OR FOOD PROCESSOR.
3. PROCESS UNTIL SMOOTH. THIN WITH RESERVED COOKING LIQUID IF NECESSARY. SHOULD BE PANCAKE BATTER CONSISTENCY. REFRIGERATE.

Rellenos
1. IN A MIXING BOWL COMBINE CHICKEN, JACK CHEESE AND BLACK BEANS. MIX WELL.
2. SLIT OPEN EACH PEPPER, STUFF WITH 3/4 CUP OF CHICKEN MIXTURE. FOLD PEPPER BACK INTO ORIGINAL SHAPE.
3. WRAP EACH PEPPER IN A PIECE OF PUFF PASTRY. FORM THE PASTRY AROUND THE PEPPER TO COVER ALL EXCEPT THE STEM (IF APPLICABLE).
4. MIX EGG WITH MILK AND BRUSH ON EDGES OF PASTRY TO SEAL.

5. FRY OR BAKE ACCORDING TO YOUR PREFERENCE:
   Frying: HEAT ENOUGH OIL TO 2" DEPTH IN POT. FRY PEPPERS, TURN TO COOK EVENLY ON ALL SIDES UNTIL CRISP AND GOLDEN BROWN. REMOVE TO PAPER TOWEL-LINED PLATE AND KEEP WARM IN OVEN UNTIL ALL ARE FRIED.

   Baking: PLACE IN PREHEATED 400° OVEN FOR 12-15 MINUTES UNTIL PASTRY IS PUFFED AND BROWNED AND PEPPERS ARE HEATED THROUGH.
6. SERVE WITH TOMATILLO-AVOCADO SALSA OVER THE TOP.

   * Canned whole green chiles (slit down the side and stuffed) may be substituted.

Ingredients:

Tomatillo-Avocado Salsa
1/2 LB. TOMATILLOS, HUSKS REMOVED & WASHED

2 CUPS WATER

2 RIPE AVOCADOS

1 JALAPEÑO PEPPER, MINCED

1/2 CUP GREEN ONIONS, RINSED & CHOPPED

1 CUP FRESH CILANTRO, RINSED & CHOPPED

1/4 CUP SOUR CREAM

2 TSP. SALT

Rellenos
2 LBS. GRILLED CHICKEN, DICED

1 1/2 CUP JACK CHEESE

1 1/2 CUPS COOKED BLACK BEANS, RINSED & COLD

12 SMALL POBLANO PEPPERS, ROASTED, PEELED & SEEDED *

1 1/2 LBS. PUFF PASTRY, ROLLED THIN & CUT INTO 12 SQUARES (5" X 5" EACH)

1 LARGE EGG

1 CUP MILK

VEGETABLE OIL FOR FRYING

SERVES: 6

VENISON POSOLE

Ingredients:

6 (8 OZ.) VENISON OSSO
    BUCCO (OR VENISON
    STEW MEAT*)

1 TSP. SALT

1 TSP. FRESH-GROUND
    BLACK PEPPER

1/4 CUP VEGETABLE OIL

2 CUPS YELLOW ONION,
    CHOPPED

3 CLOVES FRESH GARLIC,
    MINCED

2 QTS. WELL SEASONED
    BEEF STOCK

2 CUPS CANNED MEXICAN
    STYLE HOMINY,
    DRAINED

1 CUP RED BELL PEPPER,
    1" DICE

1/2 CUP POBLANO PEPPER,
    FINELY DICED

2 ANCHO CHILES,
    TOASTED & GROUND

1 CUP ROMA TOMATOES,
    LARGE DICE

1/4 CUP FRESH-SQUEEZED
    LIME JUICE

SALT & PEPPER TO TASTE

Directions:

1. SEASON VENISON WITH SALT AND PEPPER.
2. HEAT OIL IN A LARGE DUTCH OVEN AND BROWN THE VENISON ON ALL SIDES.
3. ADD THE ONION AND GARLIC AND CONTINUE TO SAUTÉ FOR ABOUT 5 MINUTES.
4. ADD THE STOCK AND BRING TO A BOIL. REDUCE HEAT AND SIMMER COVERED FOR ABOUT 2 HOURS OR UNTIL VERY TENDER. SKIM OFF ANY SURFACE FAT BEFORE ADDING REMAINING INGREDIENTS.
5. ADD HOMINY, RED PEPPER, POBLANO PEPPER, GROUND ANCHOS, ROMA TOMATOES AND LIME JUICE.
6. SIMMER POSOLE FOR ABOUT 20 MINUTES OR UNTIL THE HOMINY STARTS TO ABSORB THE FLAVOR OF THE SAUCE AND IT THICKENS SLIGHTLY.
7. TASTE AND ADJUST WITH SALT AND PEPPER AS NEEDED.

Traditional Garnishes

1 CUP SLICED RADISHES, CRISPED IN ICE WATER

1/4 HEAD GREEN CABBAGE, THINLY SHREDDED

3 AVOCADOS, SLICED

6 LIME WEDGES

WARM CORN OR FLOUR TORTILLAS

8. SERVE IN BIG BOWLS, GARNISHED WITH AVOCADO SLICES, RADISHES, CABBAGE AND A LIME WEDGE.
9. HAVE PLENTY OF WARM TORTILLAS ON HAND TO GO WITH THE STEW.

* If venison is unavailable, veal, lamb or pork may be substituted.

Noche Buena Salad

Directions:

1. Core and thinly slice or dice unpeeled apples. Soak in lemon water until ready to use.

2. Cut peel and pith off oranges. Slice thinly into rounds.

3. Peel and core pineapple, thinly slice into half-moons.

4. Mix greens together and place on a round platter.

5. Working from the outside in, make concentric circles starting with oranges, then green apples, then pineapples, then red apples. Add beets to the inner circle.

6. Chill, covered, until ready to serve.

7. When ready to serve, whisk dressing ingredients.

8. Slice banana and place in the center. Drizzle with the dressing.

9. Cut pomegranate in half and pick out the fleshy, edible seeds (meat) with a fork, being careful not to puncture.

10. Sprinkle on the pomegranate seeds and the peanuts.

11. Serve immediately.

Ingredients:

2 large Granny Smith apples

2 large red apples

2 tbsp. lemon juice (mix with 2 tbsp. water for apples)

2 large oranges

2 cups arugula

4 cups spinach, in bite size pieces

$1/2$ whole pineapple

2 cups canned beets, sliced

Dressing

$1/4$ cup orange juice

2 tbsp. lime juice

$1/2$ cup olive oil

1 tsp. sugar

$1/2$ tsp. salt

1 banana

1 cup pomegranate seeds

$1/4$ cup roasted peanuts, crushed lightly to separate halves

SERVES: 6

Fire-Grilled Turkey Skewers with Papaya-Mango Salsa & Cucumber-Mint Dipping Sauce

Ingredients:

Marinade

$1/2$ CUP BROWN SUGAR

1 CAN (7 OZ.) CHIPOTLE PEPPERS

1 TBSP. FRESH-GROUND BLACK PEPPER

$1/2$ CUP KETCHUP

1 TBSP. GROUND CUMIN

1 TSP. KOSHER SALT (OR TO TASTE)

$1/2$ CUP SOY SAUCE

$1/2$ CUP OLIVE OIL

$1/2$ CUP FRESH-SQUEEZED LIME JUICE

1 CUP WATER

3 LBS. TURKEY BREAST CUTLETS

24 (10") WOODEN SKEWERS (SOAKED IN HOT WATER FOR ABOUT AN HOUR)

Directions:

1. MIX MARINADE INGREDIENTS IN BLENDER AND PURÉE UNTIL SMOOTH. TASTE FOR SEASONINGS AND ADJUST SALT IF NECESSARY.

2. RESERVE 1 CUP FOR GLAZING AND POUR THE REST INTO A ZIPPER-CLOSE PLASTIC BAG.

3. SLICE TURKEY CUTLETS INTO 24 (1" X 4") LONG STRIPS. PLACE IN MARINADE.

4. MARINATE FOR A MINIMUM OF 4 HOURS OR OVERNIGHT.

5. REMOVE STRIPS FROM MARINADE AND THREAD ONTO SKEWERS. DISCARD MARINADE.

6. GRILL TURKEY SKEWERS OVER A MEDIUM-HOT FIRE OR GRILL UNTIL COOKED THROUGH, GLAZING WITH RESERVED MARINADE.

7. SERVE 4 PER PERSON WITH PAPAYA-MANGO SALSA AND CUCUMBER-MINT DIPPING SAUCE (PAGE 81).

**FIRE-GRILLED TURKEY SKEWERS WITH
PAPAYA-MANGO SALSA & CUCUMBER-MINT DIPPING SAUCE (CONT.)**

SERVES: 6

Directions:

Papaya-Mango Salsa
1. MIX INGREDIENTS TOGETHER AND CHILL. SERVE WITH FIRE-GRILLED TURKEY SKEWERS.

Cucumber-Mint Dipping Sauce
1. MIX INGREDIENTS TOGETHER AND CHILL. SERVE WITH FIRE-GRILLED TURKEY SKEWERS.

Ingredients:

Papaya-Mango Salsa

1 CUP PAPAYA, $1/2$" DICE

1 CUP PINEAPPLE, $1/2$" DICE

1 CUP MANGO, $1/2$" DICE

1 TBSP. FRESH CILANTRO, CHOPPED

1 TBSP. SUGAR

A PINCH OF SALT

$1/4$ CUP FRESH-SQUEEZED LIME JUICE

Cucumber-Mint Dipping Sauce

1 CUP PLAIN YOGURT

1 CUP SOUR CREAM

2 TBSP. MINT LEAVES, CHOPPED

1 LARGE CUCUMBER, GRATED & SQUEEZED DRY

$1/2$ TSP. KOSHER SALT

$1/2$ TSP. FRESH-GROUND BLACK PEPPER

2 TBSP. FRESH-SQUEEZED LIME JUICE

SERVES: 6

BRAISED BUFFALO SHORT RIBS IN MUSTARD MOLE SAUCE

Ingredients:

5 LBS. BUFFALO
    SHORT RIBS

2 TBSP. SALT

2 TBSP. FRESH-GROUND
    BLACK PEPPER

1/4 CUP VEGETABLE OIL

2 CUPS ONION, COARSELY
    CHOPPED

1 CUP CARROT, DICED

1/4 CUP MASA HARINA

2 CUPS RED WINE

2 QTS. BEEF STOCK

3 DRIED GUAJILLO CHILES

1/4 CUP RAISINS

1/4 CUP PINE NUTS

3 TBSP. DIJON MUSTARD

Directions:

1. SEASON ALL EXTERIOR SIDES OF BUFFALO RIBS WITH SALT
   AND PEPPER.

2. HEAT OIL TO MEDIUM-HIGH IN A DUTCH OVEN AND BROWN
   RIBS ON ALL SIDES.

3. ADD ONIONS, CARROTS AND MASA HARINA.

4. CONTINUE TO SAUTÉ AND STIR FOR ABOUT 5 MINUTES.

5. ADD RED WINE, BEEF STOCK, GUAJILLO CHILIES, RAISINS,
   PINE NUTS.

6. BRING TO A BOIL AND REDUCE AND COVER. SIMMER FOR
   ABOUT 2-3 HOURS OR UNTIL VERY TENDER.

7. REMOVE RIBS AND SET ASIDE.

8. IN A BLENDER, PURÉE THE REMAINING STOCK WITH SOLIDS
   AND MUSTARD TO MAKE A THICK SAUCE.

9. PLACE THE RIBS BACK IN SAUCE AND REHEAT. CUT BETWEEN
   RIBS AND SERVE.

GUAJILLO CHILES

Usually only found dry. Guajillo
chiles have a citrusy flavor and are
well suited for seafood. They are
medium hot in spice with shiny, thin
red walls, usually 5"- 6" in length.

MINI BUÑUELO SUNDAE BAR

SERVES: 12

Directions:

1. MIX CINNAMON AND SUGAR IN A BOWL AND SET ASIDE.

2. USING A 3" ROUND CUTTER, CUT OUT LITTLE TORTILLAS FROM LARGE ONES (APPROX. 4-5 PER TORTILLA).

3. HEAT OIL TO 2" DEPTH IN A SAUCEPAN AND FRY THE LITTLE TORTILLAS, SHAPING THEM INTO A CUP SHAPE WITH A WHISK OR LADLE.

4. CAREFULLY REMOVE FROM HEAT WITH A STRAINER TO DRAIN. WHILE STILL WARM, DUST WITH THE CINNAMON-SUGAR MIXTURE.

Dessert Bar

1. ARRANGE THE SUNDAE BAR WITH THE BUÑUELO SHELLS, AND AN ASSORTMENT OF ICE CREAMS WITH MINIATURE SCOOPS. ADD BOWLS OF DIFFERENT TOPPINGS, LIKE CHOCOLATE FUDGE, CARAMEL, RASPBERRY, FRESH BERRIES, CHIPS AND NUTS.

2. TOP OFF WITH FRESHLY WHIPPED CREAM AND, FOR ADULTS, SOME RASPBERRY, COFFEE OR HAZELNUT LIQUEURS.

Ingredients:

1 TBSP. GROUND CINNAMON

1 TBSP. SUGAR

12 (10") FLOUR TORTILLAS, CUT IN 3" CIRCLES

OIL FOR FRYING AS NEEDED

AN ASSORTMENT OF YOUR FAVORITE ICE CREAMS & TOPPINGS

Sunburst Squash Soup

Warm Green Bean & Mushroom Salad
with Roasted-Garlic Bleu Cheese Vinaigrette

Stuffed Turkey Rolls with
Poblano Cornbread-Chorizo Stuffing
& Pecan Mole Sauce

Smashed Candied Sweet Potatoes

Cranberry-Jalapeño Chutney

Pumpkin Crème Brulée

Thanksgiving

The Autumn harvest is the natural time to enjoy Earth's
bounty. Practically every culture has some sort of ritual
to celebrate the many beautiful foods nature provides.
This meal brings an American Southwest flavor to some
traditional dishes.

Begin your festivities with our colorful *Sunburst Squash Soup*
and *Warm Green Bean and Mushroom Salad with Roasted-Garlic
Blue Cheese Vinaigrette*. The main course of *Stuffed Turkey Rolls
with Poblano Cornbread-Chorizo Stuffing* and *Pecan Mole Sauce*
with *Smashed Candied Sweet Potatoes* and *Cranberry-Jalapeno
Chutney* is a delicious alternative to standard Thanksgiving
fare. *Pumpkin Crème Brulée* completes the experience in style.

SUNBURST SQUASH SOUP

SERVES: 6

Directions:

1. HEAT OIL IN A SOUP POT AND SAUTÉ ONIONS UNTIL TRANSLUCENT. DO NOT BROWN.

2. ADD SQUASH CUBES AND SPICES AND TOSS TO COAT.

3. ADD STOCK, BRING TO A BOIL AND REDUCE HEAT. COVER AND COOK JUST UNTIL TENDER.

4. STRAIN AND RESERVE STOCK.

5. IN A FOOD PROCESSOR OR WITH A HAND MIXER, PURÉE SOUP WITH ENOUGH STOCK TO MAKE A MEDIUM-THICK SOUP.

6. ADD CREAM AND STIR TO HEAT WELL.

7. ADD BUTTER AND ADJUST SEASONINGS IF NECESSARY.

8. KEEP ON LOW—DO NOT ALLOW TO BOIL FROM THIS POINT. IF IT GETS TOO HOT THE SOUP MAY SEPARATE.

Serve dotted with your favorite green and red bottled hot sauces pulled out from the center to form a sunburst.

Ingredients:

2 TSP. OLIVE OIL

1 LB. YELLOW ONIONS, DICED

3 LBS. BANANA SQUASH, PEELED & CUBED

$1/4$ TSP. GROUND CINNAMON

$1/4$ TSP. GROUND NUTMEG

$1/4$ TSP. GROUND ALLSPICE

$1/2$ TSP. WHITE PEPPER

$1/2$ TSP. GROUND CUMIN

2 TSP. SALT (OR TO TASTE)

$1 1/2$ QTS. CHICKEN OR VEGETABLE STOCK

1 CUP HEAVY CREAM

2 TSP. BUTTER

Serves: 6

Warm Green Bean & Mushroom Salad with Roasted-Garlic Bleu Cheese Vinaigrette

Ingredients:

Vinaigrette
1/2 CUP RED WINE VINEGAR
1/2 CUP RICE VINEGAR
1/2 CUP WATER
1/4 CUP DIJON MUSTARD
1/2 CUP ROASTED GARLIC CLOVES
1 TBSP. FRESH GARLIC, MINCED
1 TSP. SALT
1/2 TSP. FRESH-GROUND BLACK PEPPER
1 TSP. SUGAR
1/2 TSP. HERBS DE PROVENCE OR ITALIAN BLEND

1 CUP OLIVE OIL

1/2 CUP OLIVE OIL, RESERVED
1/2 LB. BLEU CHEESE

Salad
2 LBS. FRESH GREEN STRING BEANS CLEANED & SNAPPED IN HALF
6 STRIPS BACON, CUT INTO 1/2" PIECES
2 CUPS BUTTON MUSHROOMS WASHED & CUT IN QUARTERS
4 OZ. VINAIGRETTE

Directions:

Roasted-Garlic Bleu Cheese Vinaigrette (Yield: 3 1/2 cups)

1. Place vinegars, water, mustard, roasted garlic (peeled and roasted 8-12 minutes), fresh garlic and spices in a blender.

2. Blend on high until puréed.

3. With blender on medium, slowly pour in a thin stream of oil through the hole in the lid.

4. Blend until emulsified. Pour into a jar with a tight fitting lid.

5. Add the bleu cheese crumbles and the reserved oil. Shake well.

6. Chill vinaigrette for 2 hours to allow the flavors to bloom.

7. Shake well each time you use and ladle dressing, including some chunks of cheese.

Note: This tastes best if you let the vinaigrette sit out to bring it back to room temperature rather than serving it ice cold.

Salad

1. Blanch the beans in salted, boiling water for 2 minutes. Remove from water and quickly cool down in an ice bath. (These can be done in advance and stored in refrigerator.)

2. In a heavy sauté pan, cook the bacon until crispy. Remove from heat. Reserve 3 tbsp. of bacon fat in the pan and discard the rest. Sauté mushrooms in bacon fat for 5 minutes until lightly browned. Add blanched green beans and toss to reheat, about 4-5 minutes.

3. Place in serving bowl and toss with the vinaigrette.

4. Serve warm.

STUFFED TURKEY ROLLS WITH POBLANO CORNBREAD-CHORIZO STUFFING & PECAN MOLE SAUCE

SERVES: 6-8

Directions:

1. REMOVE TENDON FROM TENDERLOINS, SPLITTING IN TWO. BUTTERFLY EACH PIECE OPEN AND POUND SLIGHTLY TO FLATTEN AND EVEN OUT THICKNESS.

2. MIX WINE, MUSTARD, SEASONINGS AND OIL IN A ZIPPER-CLOSE PLASTIC BAG AND ADD TENDERLOIN FILLETS.

3. MARINATE FOR A MINIMUM OF 2 HOURS OR OVERNIGHT.

4. REMOVE FROM MARINADE AND DISCARD BAG. LAY TENDERLOINS OUT FLAT ON A WORK SURFACE.

5. STUFF WITH POBLANO CORNBREAD-CHORIZO STUFFING (PAGE 88), ROLLING OVER TO ENCLOSE.

6. LAY TURKEY ROLLS SEAM-SIDE DOWN IN A BUTTERED BAKING DISH.

7. ADD ANY LEFT OVER STUFFING TO THE ENDS OF THE ROLLS.

8. POUR IN 1 CUP OF STOCK AND COVER.

9. BAKE AT 325° FOR ABOUT AN HOUR OR UNTIL DONE IN MIDDLE.

10. SERVE WITH PECAN MOLE SAUCE (PAGE 88).

Ingredients:

4 TURKEY TENDERLOINS (ABOUT 2 LBS. TOTAL)

Marinade

1 CUP WHITE WINE

3 TBSP. DIJON MUSTARD

1/2 TSP. SALT

1 TSP. FRESH-GROUND BLACK PEPPER

1 TBSP. MUSTANG SPICE™

1 TSP. POULTRY SEASONING OR MIXED HERBS

1/2 CUP OLIVE OIL

1 CUP CHICKEN STOCK

1 RECIPE POBLANO CORNBREAD-CHORIZO STUFFING

1 RECIPE PECAN MOLE SAUCE

MUSTANG SPICE™

Mustang Spice™ is available from your favorite Canyon Cafe, Sam's Cafe, or Desert Fire Restaurants. You may make your own by using 1/2 cup each of New Mexican Red Chile Powder and Cajun Blackening Spice and 1 Tbsp. salt.

SERVES: 6-8

Ingredients:

Poblano Stuffing

1 9" X 9" PAN CORN BREAD, CRUMBLED
1/2 TSP. EACH DRIED SAGE, THYME, OREGANO & CUMIN
1 TSP. FRESH-GROUND BLACK PEPPER
1/2 TSP. SALT
2 POBLANO PEPPERS, ROASTED, PEELED, SEEDED & DICED
1/2 STICK BUTTER
1 CUP RED ONIONS, DICED
1 CUP CELERY, SLICED
1LB. CHORIZO, COOKED & WELL DRAINED
3 EGGS
2 CUPS CHICKEN STOCK (OR MORE AS NECESSARY)

Pecan Mole Sauce

2 ANCHO CHILES
2 CUPS WATER
3 TBSP. OLIVE OIL
1 CUP ONION, DICED
3 CLOVES GARLIC
4 ROMA TOMATOES
1 CUP ROASTED PECANS
2 SLICES STALE WHITE BREAD
4 CUPS CHICKEN STOCK
1/2 CUP RED WINE
1/2 TSP. GROUND CINNAMON

Directions:

Poblano Cornbread-Chorizo Stuffing

1. CRUMBLE CORNBREAD INTO BOWL. ADD HERBS, POBLANO, AND SPICES.

2. HEAT BUTTER AND SAUTE ONIONS AND CELERY UNTIL CLEAR.

3. ADD TO CORNBREAD. MIX WELL. ADD ENOUGH STOCK TO MOISTEN.

4. ADD DRAINED CHORIZO AND MIX IN WELL. BEAT EGGS AND ADD TO STUFFING.

5. USE TO STUFF TURKEY TENDERLOINS, OR TO USE AS A CASSEROLE BAKE IN A PAN ABOUT 25 MINUTES AT 350°.

Pecan Mole Sauce

1. SOAK ANCHO CHILES IN WARM WATER ABOUT 10 MINUTES TO REHYDRATE. DRAIN.

2. HEAT 1 TBSP. OF OLIVE OIL AND ADD ONIONS AND GARLIC CLOVES AND SAUTE ABOUT 8 MINUTES OR UNTIL BROWNED AND CARAMELIZED. RESERVE.

3. BROIL OR ROAST TOMATOES UNTIL SKINS ARE BLACKENED AND SLIGHTLY SOFTENED. PEEL WHEN COOL ENOUGH TO HANDLE AND DISCARD SKINS.

4. PLACE TOMATOES, PECANS, BREAD, ANCHOS AND 1 CUP OF BROTH IN A BLENDER. PROCESS UNTIL SMOOTH.

5. HEAT OIL IN A LARGE SKILLET, ADD PURÉE FROM BLENDER THEN ADD REMAINING INGREDIENTS.

6. COOK, STIRRING OCCASIONALLY UNTIL THICKENED, ABOUT 1 HOUR. STRAIN IF SMOOTHER SAUCE IS DESIRED AND SERVE.

SMASHED CANDIED SWEET POTATOES

SERVES: 6

Directions:

1. PREHEAT OVEN TO 400°.

2. ROAST POTATOES UNTIL TENDER, ABOUT 45 MINUTES.

3. LET SIT UNTIL COOL ENOUGH TO HANDLE.

4. CUT IN HALF AND SCOOP INSIDES INTO A LARGE BOWL. DISCARD THE SKINS.

5. SMASH, MIXING IN REMAINING INGREDIENTS.

6. PLACE IN A SERVING DISH AND RETURN TO OVEN TO REHEAT UNTIL HOT. SERVE HOT.

Ingredients:

5 LARGE SWEET POTATOES (ABOUT 3 LBS.)

1 CUP HONEY

2 TBSP. NEW MEXICAN RED CHILE POWDER

2 TBSP. RED WINE VINEGAR

1/2 CUP BUTTER

1 TSP. SALT

1 TBSP. FRESH-GROUND BLACK PEPPER

SERVES: 6

Ingredients:

4 CUPS FRESH OR FROZEN
   CRANBERRIES,
   ROUGHLY CHOPPED

2 FRESH JALAPEÑOS,
   THINLY SLICED

1/2 CUP GOLDEN RAISINS

1 TBPS. FRESH CILANTRO,
   FINELY CHOPPED

2 TBSP. CRYSTALLIZED
   GINGER, MINCED

2 TBSP. FRESH-SQUEEZED
   LIME JUICE

1/2 CUP CRANBERRY
   JUICE

1/2 TSP. SALT

1 CUP SUGAR

CRANBERRY-JALAPEÑO CHUTNEY

Directions:

1. COMBINE ALL INGREDIENTS AND COOK OVER MEDIUM
    HEAT UNTIL CRANBERRIES ARE TENDER AND CHUTNEY
    IS THICKENED.

2. TASTE; IF TOO TART, ADD MORE SUGAR.

3. LET COOL. COVER AND REFRIGERATE OVERNIGHT.

4. SERVE AS A GARNISH FOR THE STUFFED TURKEY ROLLS.
    THIS IS ALSO GREAT SERVED WITH PORK TENDERLOIN OR
    ROASTED TURKEY.

PUMPKIN CRÈME BRULÉE

SERVES: 6

Directions:

1. PREHEAT OVEN TO 325°.
2. SLIT VANILLA BEAN LENGTHWISE.
3. HEAT CREAM, SUGAR AND VANILLA BEAN UNTIL HOT, BUT NOT BOILING TO DISSOLVE SUGAR. REMOVE FROM HEAT.
4. MEANWHILE, BEAT EGG YOLKS, PUMPKIN, AND VANILLA EXTRACT UNTIL SMOOTH.
5. STRAIN OUT VANILLA BEAN FROM CREAM MIXTURE.
6. RESERVE BEAN AND SCRAPE OUT SEEDS. ADD SEEDS BACK TO CREAM MIXTURE AND STIR TO INCORPORATE.
7. TEMPER THE EGG YOLKS BY ADDING JUST A LITTLE OF THE HOT CREAM MIXTURE TO EQUALIZE THE TEMPERATURE. THIS WILL KEEP THE EGGS FROM "SCRAMBLING" WHEN THE REST OF THE HOT MIXTURE IS ADDED. THEN ADD THE REST OF THE CREAM AND MIX WELL.
8. POUR INTO 6 SMALL RAMEKINS. PLACE THE RAMEKINS IN A BAIN MARIE ("WATER BATH": A 2" HIGH ROASTING PAN FILLED HALFWAY UP WITH HOT WATER).
9. BAKE AT 325° FOR 20-30 MINUTES UNTIL FIRM, BUT STILL A LITTLE WIGGLY IN THE CENTER.
10. REMOVE FROM WATER AND CHILL 4 HOURS OR OVERNIGHT.
11. SIFT SUGAR ONTO TOP AND USING A TORCH OR BROILER, QUICKLY BROWN TO CARAMELIZE SUGAR.
12. GARNISH WITH A FEW RASPBERRIES OR SLICED STRAWBERRIES AND SERVE IMMEDIATELY.

Ingredients:

Custard
$1/2$ VANILLA BEAN, SPLIT

$2\,1/2$ CUPS HEAVY CREAM

$2/3$ CUP SUGAR

8 LARGE EGG YOLKS

1 CUP PUMPKIN

1 TBSP. VANILLA EXTRACT

Topping
$1/2$ CUP SUGAR

FRESH RASPBERRIES OR STRAWBERRIES FOR GARNISH

Winter Solstice Celebration
On the Plaza
Full Moon Coyote Dinner
Romantic Dinner for Two

Winter

Sedona Spring Rolls
with Chipotle BBQ Sauce

Flank Steak Maldonado &
Roasted Tomato Tequila Corn Salsa

Southwest Paella

Banana Burritos

White Chocolate Tamales

Chocolate Truffle Bites

Winter Solstice Celebration

The longest night of the year may seem depressing to some, but for many cultures, it is a celebration of the sun's return to our hemisphere. At this time of year, opportunities abound for feasts and festivities of all kinds. This menu was designed for a holiday party with a Southwest flair.

Set the stage for the perfect evening with luminaria lighting the path to your door. On a table decorated with evergreens and candles, set a hearty feast of *Sedona Spring Rolls with Chipotle BBQ Sauce, Flank Steak Maldonado with Roasted Tomato-Tequila-Corn Salsa* and savory *Southwest Paella.* Treat your guests with *Banana Burritos, White Chocolate Tamales* and *Chocolate Truffle Bites* for a lavish seasonal dessert.

SEDONA SPRING ROLLS WITH CHIPOTLE BBQ SAUCE

SERVES: 6

Directions:

1. IN A SKILLET, HEAT SESAME AND OLIVE OILS. SAUTÉ GARLIC, ONION, CABBAGE, CARROTS, AND POBLANOS. STIR-FRY OVER MEDIUM HEAT FOR 5 MINUTES.

2. REMOVE FROM HEAT. ADD CHICKEN, SPINACH, BALSAMIC VINEGAR AND SOY SAUCE.

3. SEASON WITH BLACK PEPPER AND TOSS WELL TO COAT. COOL THIS MIXTURE.

4. WARM TORTILLAS SLIGHTLY TO MAKE PLIABLE.

5. DIVIDE MIXTURE EVENLY BETWEEN EACH TORTILLA AND ROLL TIGHTLY LIKE A BURRITO, TUCKING IN SIDES.

6. SEAL ENDS WITH A LITTLE EGG YOLK.

7. HEAT 2" OIL IN A SAUCE PAN.

8. DEEP FRY SPRING ROLLS UNTIL GOLDEN BROWN (ABOUT 6 MINUTES). CUT IN HALF (ON BIAS) TO SHOW FILLING.

9. SERVE HOT, CUT SIDE UP, COVERED WITH A DRIZZLE OF CHIPOTLE BBQ SAUCE (PAGE 96).

Ingredients:

2 TBSP. SESAME OIL

1 TBSP. OLIVE OIL

1 TBSP. FRESH GARLIC, MINCED

1 CUP RED ONIONS, JULIENNED

2 CUPS RED CABBAGE, SHREDDED

1 CUP CARROTS, JULIENNED

2 POBLANO PEPPERS, JULIENNED

2 (8 OZ.) CHICKEN BREASTS, GRILLED & JULIENNED

2 CUPS SPINACH, STEMMED & SLICED

1 TSP. FRESH-GROUND BLACK PEPPER

1/4 CUP BALSAMIC VINEGAR

1/4 CUP SOY SAUCE

12 (6") FLOUR TORTILLAS

2 EGG YOLKS

OIL FOR FRYING

1 RECIPE CHIPOTLE BBQ SAUCE

SERVES: 6

Ingredients:

Chipotle BBQ Sauce

1 1/2 LBS. ROMA TOMATOES

1 LARGE ONION

6 CLOVES GARLIC

1/4 CUP CHIPOTLE PEPPERS (OR MORE TO TASTE)

1 CUP BROWN SUGAR

1/2 CUP RED WINE VINEGAR

1/2 CUP WORCESTERSHIRE SAUCE

1 TBSP. SALT

Directions:

Chipotle BBQ Sauce

1. PREHEAT OVEN TO 400°.

2. HALVE TOMATOES, QUARTER ONION AND PLACE ON A BAKING SHEET WITH GARLIC.

3. ROAST AT 400° FOR ABOUT 25 MINUTES OR UNTIL TOMATO SKINS BEGIN TO BLACKEN. DON'T PEEL.

4. PLACE IN FOOD PROCESSOR OR BLENDER WITH CHIPOTLE PEPPERS. BLEND UNTIL SMOOTH.

5. ADD ALL THE REMAINING INGREDIENTS AND MIX WELL TO INCORPORATE.

6. PLACE IN A SAUCEPAN AND COOK UNTIL SLIGHTLY REDUCED.

7. CHILL OR SERVE RIGHT AWAY.

FLANK STEAK MALDONADO & ROASTED TOMATO TEQUILA CORN SALSA

SERVES: 12

Directions:

Flank Steak Maldonado
1. PREHEAT OVEN TO 400°.
2. BUTTERFLY FLANK STEAK OPEN WITH THE GRAIN OR POUND THIN WITH A MEAT MALLET.
3. SEASON WITH SALT AND PEPPER ON BOTH SIDES.
4. LAY ROASTED RED PEPPERS OVER STEAK, TOP WITH BLANCHED SPINACH.
5. LAY CHEESE OVER SPINACH, COVERING WELL.
6. LAY POBLANO STRIPS OVER CHEESE.
7. ROLL UP TIGHTLY LIKE A JELLY ROLL.
8. TIE WITH TWINE.
9. HEAT A SMALL AMOUNT OF OIL IN A SKILLET AND BROWN ROLLS QUICKLY.
10. PLACE IN OVEN AND ROAST AT 400° FOR 15 MINUTES FOR MEDIUM RARE
11. REMOVE FROM OVEN AND LET REST 5 MINUTES.
12. REMOVE STRINGS AND CUT EACH INTO NEAT SLICES ON THE BIAS.
13. SERVE WITH ROASTED TOMATO TEQUILA CORN SALSA (PAGE 98).

Ingredients:

Flank Steak Maldonado
2 LBS. FLANK STEAK, BUTTERFLIED OR POUNDED THINLY

1/2 TSP. SALT

1/2 TSP. FRESH-GROUND BLACK PEPPER

1 CUP RED BELL PEPPERS, ROASTED, PEELED & SEEDED

1 LB. SPINACH, CLEANED, BLANCHED & SQUEEZED DRY

8 OZ. PEPPER JACK CHEESE, SLICED

1 CUP POBLANO PEPPERS, ROASTED, PEELED, SEEDED & CUT INTO STRIPS

YIELD: 4 CUPS

FLANK STEAK MALDONADO & ROASTED TOMATO TEQUILA CORN SALSA (CONT.)

Ingredients:

**Roasted Tomato
Tequila Corn Salsa**

1/2 LB. ROMA TOMATOES

1/4 CUP GARLIC CLOVES

2 EARS FRESH CORN

1 LARGE YELLOW ONION,
   QUARTERED

1/2 CUP CHIPOTLE
   PEPPERS (7 OZ. CAN)

2 OZ. GOLD TEQUILA

1 TBSP. OREGANO

1 TBSP. ACHIOTE PASTE

2 TSP. FRESH-GROUND
   BLACK PEPPER

1/2 CUP CHICKEN STOCK

Directions:

Roasted Tomato Tequila Corn Salsa

1. PREHEAT OVEN TO 400°.

2. PLACE TOMATOES, GARLIC, CORN AND ONIONS ON A BAKING SHEET AND ROAST ABOUT 20 MINUTES AT 400°.

3. FINELY DICE ROASTED ONIONS AND CUT CORN FROM THE COB.

4. PLACE TOMATOES, CHIPOTLES AND GARLIC IN FOOD PROCESSOR AND THICKLY PURÉE. REMOVE AND PLACE IN A SAUCE POT.

5. ADD TEQUILA, ROASTED CORN, ONIONS AND SPICES.

6. HEAT UNTIL BOILING. KEEP WARM UNTIL SERVING.

7. SERVE WITH THE STUFFED FLANK STEAK MALDONADO. THIS SALSA IS ALSO WONDERFUL SERVED WITH FISH, CHICKEN OR BEEF OR USED AS A PASTA OR PIZZA SAUCE.

ACHIOTE PASTE

Seeds of the Annatto Tree from Central America that have been ground into a moist paste which is usually sold in bricks. Adds a distinct but non-spicy flavor to classic dishes. It is what gives cheddar cheese its trademark color and is also used to color butter.

SOUTHWEST PAELLA

SERVES: 12

Directions:

1. COMBINE BUTTER, GARLIC AND PARSLEY. MELT IN ONE OR TWO LARGE SHALLOW SKILLETS OR PAELLA PANS.

2. ADD CHORIZO AND FRY UNTIL ALMOST CRISPY. ADD RICE AND SAUTE 3-4 MINUTES.

3. ADD CHICKEN STOCK AND SAFFRON. BRING TO A BOIL. REDUCE HEAT, COVER AND COOK FOR 15 MINUTES.

4. WHEN RICE IS ALMOST TENDER AND MOST OF THE LIQUID ABSORBED, ARRANGE THE LOBSTER TAILS, MUSSELS AND SHRIMP AROUND THE PAN.

5. ADD CHICKEN TO PAN, BURYING IT IN THE RICE.

6. COVER AND PLACE THE ENTIRE DISH INTO THE OVEN TO HEAT THOROUGHLY AND FINISH COOKING THE SHELLFISH AND RICE, ABOUT 10 MINUTES.

7. UNCOVER AND GARNISH WITH THE CHOPPED FRESH TOMATO AND CILANTRO.

* Whole crawfish can be substituted for lobster, and clams for mussels or different seafood can be combined to your liking.

Ingredients:

4 OZ. BUTTER

2 TBSP. FRESH GARLIC, MINCED

2 TBSP. PARSLEY, MINCED

2 LB. CHORIZO SAUSAGE, CUT IN 1" PIECES

6 CUPS SHORT GRAIN RICE, RINSED TWICE

3 QTS. CHICKEN STOCK, WELL SEASONED

2 TSP. SAFFRON STRANDS, DISSOLVED IN STOCK

6 SMALL LOBSTER TAILS, IN SHELL & SPLIT IN TWO*

4 DOZEN FRESH MUSSELS*

2 LB. RAW MEDIUM SHRIMP

2 WHOLE ROASTED CHICKENS, CUT IN QUARTERS

Garnish

2 CUPS DICED TOMATO, CUT INTO 1" PIECES

4 TBSP. FRESH CILANTRO, CHOPPED FINE FOR GARNISH

SERVES: 6

BANANA BURRITOS & WHITE CHOCOLATE TAMALES

Ingredients:

Banana Burritos
6 BANANAS

2 TSP. GROUND CINNAMON

1/2 CUP CHOCOLATE
    CHIPS

12 PHYLLO DOUGH
    SHEETS

1/2 CUP BUTTER, MELTED

White Chocolate Tamales
12 DRIED CORN HUSKS

8 OZ. WHITE CHOCOLATE
    CHIPS

3/4 CUP ROASTED PECANS,
    MINCED

Directions:

Banana Burritos
1. PREHEAT OVEN TO 400°.
2. PEEL AND ROLL BANANAS IN CINNAMON THEN IN CHOCOLATE CHIPS.
3. LAY OUT PHYLLO SHEETS AND BUTTER ONE, THEN STACK ANOTHER ON TOP AND BUTTER IT.
4. PLACE COVERED BANANAS ON PREPARED PHYLLO SHEETS AND ROLL UP BURRITO STYLE, TUCKING IN THE ENDS TO MAKE A TIGHT PACKAGE.
5. BRUSH WITH MORE BUTTER AND PLACE ON BAKING SHEET.
6. FINISH REMAINING BANANAS.
7. BAKE AT 400° UNTIL LIGHTLY BROWNED.
8. REMOVE FROM OVEN AND CUT IN HALF (ON BIAS).
9. SERVE WITH ICE CREAM AND CHOCOLATE SAUCE. SPRINKLE WITH PECANS.

White Chocolate Tamales
1. SOAK HUSKS TO MAKE PLIABLE IN WARM WATER. DRAIN AND DRY WELL. TEAR INTO 1 1/2" WIDE STRIPS. RESERVE
2. MELT WHITE CHOCOLATE CHIPS IN A DOUBLE BOILER. WHEN COMPLETELY MELTED, STIR IN PECANS.
3. TAKE A TBSP. OF THE MIXTURE AND SPREAD DOWN THE LENGTH OF THE HUSK.
4. WRAP UP LIKE A TAMALE AND PLACE ON A SHEET PAN.
5. CHILL TO SET THEN STORE IN AN AIRTIGHT CONTAINER IN A COOL PLACE.

CHOCOLATE TRUFFLE BITES

SERVES: 6-8

Directions:

1. HEAT CREAM TO NEAR BOILING. CHOP UNSWEETENED CHOCOLATE AND PLACE IN A BOWL WITH CHIPS.

2. POUR CREAM ONTO CHOCOLATES AND LET REST 5 MINUTES. STIR TO MELT.

3. ADD BUTTER IN CUBES AND WHISK TO MELT.

4. ADD YOLKS AND LIGHTLY WHISK TO MIX. DO NOT OVER WHIP. RESERVE.

5. MIX CRUMBS WITH MELTED BUTTER AND SPREAD IN A 9" X 13" BAKING PAN. PRESS EVENLY.

6. POUR AND SPREAD TRUFFLE MIXTURE OVER THE CRUMBS.

7. REFRIGERATE FOR A MINIMUM OF 4 HOURS OR OVERNIGHT.

8. CUT INTO LITTLE SQUARES AND SERVE.

9. THESE LOOK GREAT DRIZZLED WITH MELTED WHITE OR MILK CHOCOLATE.

Ingredients:

3 CUPS HEAVY CREAM

4 OZ. UNSWEETENED BAKING CHOCOLATE

1 1/2 LBS. SEMI SWEET CHOCOLATE CHIPS

4 OZ. BUTTER

4 EGG YOLKS

3 CUPS CHOCOLATE COOKIE CRUMBS

1/2 CUP BUTTER, MELTED

WHITE OR MILK CHOCOLATE, MELTED, FOR GARNISH (OPTIONAL)

Queso Fresco & Scallion
Empanadas with Field Greens

Chicken Fried Tuna Steak
with Jalapeño Cream Gravy

Chile Mashed Potatoes

Calabasitas

Sweet Potato & Pecan
Empanadas

On the Plaza

Perhaps the most appealing features of American Southwest
architecture are the secluded plazas and courtyards which
are as much a part of the living space as any interior room.
In the northern part of the Southwest, Winter's periodic
snowfalls blanket these hidden sanctuaries with white,
setting a mood that is ideal for an early dinner in the
company of friends.

This meal begins with *Queso Fresco and Scallion Empanadas* on
a bed of *Field Greens with Honey-Chipotle Vinaigrette*, followed
by *Chicken Fried Tuna Steak with Jalapeno Gravy*, *Chile Mashed
Potatoes* and *Calabasitas*. Complete the evening with warm
Sweet Potato and Pecan Empanadas in front of a roaring fire.

Queso Fresco & Scallion Empanadas with Field Greens

SERVES: 6

Directions:

1. Roll out pie pastry and cut into 6 thin circles about 3 1/2" across.

2. Crumble queso fresco and, using a fork, mix with cream cheese. (This mixture will not be smooth.)

3. Mix in scallions. Divide mixture evenly on the 6 pastry circles and fold over to form half-moon empanadas. Crimp edges with a fork to seal.

4. Heat enough oil in a pan to come to 2" depth. Turning once, fry empanadas until golden brown on both sides and heated through.

5. Toss field greens with honey-chipotle vinaigrette and divide on 6 plates.

6. Add one empanada and half of an avocado, peeled and fanned to each plate.

7. Garnish with diced tomato.

   * See page 73 for Honey-Chipotle Vinaigrette recipe.

Ingredients:

1 RECIPE DOUBLE
    CRUST PASTRY

8 OZ. QUESO FRESCO

4 OZ. CREAM CHEESE

4 SCALLIONS, THINLY
    SLICED

OIL FOR FRYING
    AS NEEDED

6 CUPS FIELD GREENS

6 TBSP. HONEY-CHIPOTLE
    VINAIGRETTE*

3 AVOCADOS

3 ROMA TOMATOES,
    DICED & SEEDED

EMPANADAS

Crisp pastries in the shape of half-moons. They can be savory or sweet, small or large. Can be stuffed with a variety of fillings and then baked or fried. Similar to a turn-over.

SERVES: 6

CHICKEN FRIED TUNA STEAK WITH JALAPEÑO CREAM GRAVY

Ingredients:

2 CUPS FLOUR

1 TSP. SALT

1 TSP. FRESH-GROUND
   BLACK PEPPER

2 CUPS MILK

2 LARGE EGGS

6 (6 OZ.) FRESH TUNA
   STEAKS, $1/2$" - $3/4$"
   THICK

OIL FOR FRYING
   AS NEEDED

Jalapeño Cream Gravy

1 TBSP. BUTTER

$1/2$ CUP ONION, $1/4$" DICE

1 TSP. FRESH GARLIC,
   MINCED

2 LARGE SLICED
   JALAPEÑOS
   (OR TO TASTE)

2 CUPS HEAVY CREAM

$1/2$ TSP. FRESH-GROUND
   BLACK PEPPER

1 TSP. SALT

1 PINCH CAYENNE

$1/4$ CUP BLOND ROUX

$1/2$ CUP MILK (IF NEEDED)

Directions:

1. SEASON FLOUR WITH SALT AND PEPPER, DISTRIBUTING SPICES WELL.
2. BEAT EGGS WITH MILK.
3. DREDGE TUNA STEAKS IN SEASONED FLOUR. THEN DIP INTO THE EGG MIXTURE, THEN BACK INTO THE FLOUR.
4. REPEAT UNTIL ALL STEAKS ARE DONE.
5. PAN-FRY IN 1" OIL OR DEEP-FRY AT $350°$ FOR ABOUT 2-3 MINUTES A SIDE OR UNTIL TUNA IS COOKED THROUGH. DRAIN WELL AND KEEP WARM UNTIL ALL STEAKS ARE FRIED.
6. TOP TUNA STEAK WITH 4 OZ. OF JALAPEÑO GRAVY AND SERVE WITH CHILE MASHED POTATOES (PAGE 107) AND VEGETABLES OF YOUR CHOICE.
7. WE LIKE TO ADD A FRESH JALAPEÑO FOR GARNISH ON THE STEAK.

Jalapeño Cream Gravy

1. MELT BUTTER AND SAUTÉ ONIONS AND GARLIC 2-3 MINUTES OVER MEDIUM FLAME. DO NOT BROWN!
2. ADD JALAPEÑOS, CREAM AND SEASONINGS AND COOK UNTIL ONIONS ARE SOFT.
3. MAKE A $1/4$ CUP OF BLOND ROUX BY COOKING EQUAL PARTS OF UNSALTED BUTTER AND FLOUR ($1/2$ STICK BUTTER AND $1/4$ CUP FLOUR) FOR 5 MINUTES OVER MEDIUM HEAT UNTIL BLOND COLORED BUT NOT BROWNED. THIS CAN BE MADE IN A LARGER BATCH, AND KEPT REFRIGERATED FOR LATER USE.
4. WHISK ROUX INTO CREAM, TAKING CARE TO DISSOLVE ANY LUMPS.
5. COOK 5-6 MINUTES UNTIL THE STARCHY TASTE DISAPPEARS AND GRAVY IS THICKENED.
6. TASTE AND ADJUST SEASONINGS IF NECESSARY. THIN WITH A LITTLE MILK IF TOO THICK.
7. SERVE HOT OVER THE CHICKEN FRIED TUNA. THIS ALSO MAKES A GREAT PASTA SAUCE.

CHILE MASHED POTATOES

SERVES: 6-8

Directions:

1. BOIL POTATOES IN WATER UNTIL TENDER.

2. BOIL CARROTS SEPARATELY UNTIL JUST TENDER. DRAIN AND RESERVE TO ADD AFTER POTATOES ARE MASHED.

3. PLACE POTATOES IN A LARGE BOWL OR MIXER AND BEGIN MASHING.

4. ADD BUTTER AND SOUR CREAM. WHIP UNTIL FLUFFY.

5. ADD REMAINING INGREDIENTS AND MIX IN WELL.

6. TASTE AND ADJUST SALT AND PEPPER IF NECESSARY.

   Mild canned green chiles can be substituted if desired.

Ingredients:

4 LBS. NEW POTATOES, CUBED

1 LARGE CARROT, $1/2$" DICE

2 STICKS BUTTER

1 CUP SOUR CREAM

$1/2$ BUNCH GREEN ONIONS, TRIMMED & SLICED

2 POBLANO PEPPERS,* ᶫ ROASTED, PEELED, SEEDED & DICED

2 TSP. SALT

1 TSP. FRESH-GROUND BLACK PEPPER

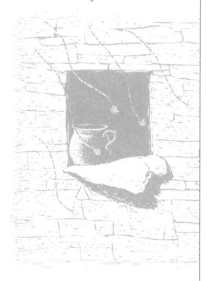

SERVES: 6

Ingredients:

- 2 CUPS ZUCCHINI
- 2 CUPS RED BELL PEPPER
- 2 CUPS BUTTERNUT SQUASH
- 1/2 CUP EXTRA VIRGIN OLIVE OIL
- 2 CUPS FRESH CORN
- 1 TSP. SALT (OR TO TASTE)
- 1 TSP. FRESH-GROUND BLACK PEPPER (OR TO TASTE)
- 1 TBSP. FRESH GARLIC, MINCED
- 1 BAG (10 OZ.) SPINACH LEAVES, STEMMED

CALABASITAS

Directions:

1. PREHEAT OVEN TO 400°.
2. CUT ZUCCHINI AND RED PEPPER INTO 1/2" CUBES.
3. PEEL BUTTERNUT SQUASH. CUT INTO 1/2" CUBES.
4. BLANCH BUTTERNUT SQUASH IN BOILING WATER FOR 4-5 MINUTES. DRAIN.
5. TOSS 1/4 CUP OLIVE OIL, ZUCCHINI, RED PEPPER, CORN, AND BUTTERNUT SQUASH IN A LARGE BOWL. SEASON WITH SALT, PEPPER AND GARLIC.
6. SPREAD EVENLY ONTO A BAKING SHEET.
7. COOK AT 400° FOR 13-15 MINUTES.
8. IN LARGE SAUTE PAN, HEAT REMAINING OLIVE OIL. ADD BAKED VEGETABLES AND TOSS IN SPINACH. COOK OVER MEDIUM HEAT JUST UNTIL SPINACH BEGINS TO WILT.
9. SERVE HOT OR AT ROOM TEMPERATURE.

CALABASITAS

A traditional squash dish, usually made of a green Mexican squash stewed with green pepper, onion, jalapeños, corn and tomatoes. Our version is a new interpretation of an old favorite.

SWEET POTATO & PECAN EMPANADAS

SERVES: 6

Directions:

1. PREHEAT OVEN TO 350°.
2. PREPARE YOUR FAVORITE PIE DOUGH RECIPE. DIVIDE INTO 6 BALLS. RESERVE.
3. PURÉE YAMS (SWEET POTATOES) IN FOOD PROCESSOR WITH SALT, 2 TBSP. OF THE SUGAR AND EGG YOLK.
4. ADD SPICES AND PECANS. MIX WELL.
5. ROLL OUT DOUGH BALLS INTO 6" CIRCLES.
6. SPREAD EACH CIRCLE WITH THE FILLING AND FOLD OVER FORMING HALF-MOONS. CRIMP EDGES WITH FORK TINES DIPPED IN SUGAR.
7. BEAT EGG WHITE WITH 1 TBSP. WATER AND BRUSH ON EMPANADAS.
8. SPRINKLE EACH WITH THE REMAINING SUGAR.
9. PLACE ON BAKING SHEET AND BAKE AT 350° UNTIL GOLDEN (ABOUT 20 MINUTES).
10. SERVE WARM.

Ingredients:

1 RECIPE DOUBLE CRUST PIE DOUGH

1 CAN (14 OZ.) YAMS, IN SYRUP (DRAINED)

1/4 TSP. SALT

1/4 CUP SUGAR

1 LARGE EGG, SEPARATED

1/4 TSP. EACH GROUND CINNAMON, ALLSPICE & CORIANDER

1/2 CUP PECANS

1 TBSP. WATER

YAMS VS. SWEET POTATOES

One variety of sweet potato is pale-skinned with yellow flesh. What we call the "yam," has dark skin and orange flesh, and is really another variety of sweet potato. True yams are not related to sweet potatoes and are rarely grown in the US. Canned "yams" can be either variety and, in different regions, the fresh vegetable can be called by either name.

Crabmeat Queso Flameado
Jack's Sliced Avocado Salad
Carne Asada
Coconut Rum Flan
Blue Moon Margaritas

Full Moon Coyote Dinner

If you have ever heard coyotes howling at a January moon, it is easy to understand why some believe that they are Nature's storyteller. Their eerie calls tell beautiful, lonely tales of chilly winter nights. This meal is perfect for a cold, clear night when the air smells of a fresh fallen snow and the moon lights a path to the sky. Build a fire in your fireplace and gather family and friends close to tell stories of your own.

Crabmeat Queso Flameado makes a grand entrance to your evening, especially when accompanied by *Jack's Sliced Avocado Salad, Carne Asada* and a creamy *Coconut-Rum Flan* for dessert. Our *Blue Moon Margaritas* add that perfect bit of cheer to the cold winter night.

CRABMEAT QUESO FLAMEADO

SERVES: 6-8

Directions:

1. HEAT BUTTER IN CAST IRON SKILLET AND SAUTÉ MUSHROOMS UNTIL LIGHTLY BROWNED.

2. ADD CRABMEAT, POBLANO STRIPS AND JALAPEÑO GRAVY. STIR TO COMBINE AND HEAT THROUGH.

3. COVER WITH ASADERO CHEESE AND PLACE IN BROILER OR OVEN TO MELT.

4. WHEN MELTED, TOP WITH ALCOHOL AND FLAME WITH A MATCH. THIS STEP IS A VISUALLY IMPRESSIVE PART OF THE PRESENTATION, BUT DOES NOTHING TO ENHANCE THE FLAVOR SO IT IS OPTIONAL.

5. SERVE SPOONED INTO WARM TORTILLAS OR DIP WITH CRISP TORTILLA CHIPS.

* See page 104 for Jalapeno Cream Gravy recipe.

ASADERO CHEESE

A fresh Mexican cheese, slightly aged and tangy in flavor. It is very good melted, used for dips, enchiladas, quesadillas and for stuffing empanadas or chile rellenos. If you can't find Asadero, Monterey Jack cheese may be substituted.

Ingredients:

2 TBSP. BUTTER

1 CUP FRESH MUSHROOMS, SLICED

6 OZ. CRABMEAT, THAWED & DRAINED

1/2 CUP POBLANO PEPPERS, ROASTED, PEELED & SLICED

4 OZ. JALAPEÑO CREAM GRAVY*

4 OZ. ASADERO CHEESE, GRATED OR SLICED

1 TBSP. GRAIN ALCOHOL (OPTIONAL, IF FLAME DESIRED)

6 (6") FLOUR TORTILLAS, WARMED & FOLDED

CRISP TORTILLA CHIPS

SERVES: 6

JACK'S SLICED AVOCADO SALAD

Ingredients:

Wheat Beer Dressing

$^1/_4$ CUP WHEAT BEER

1 BAY LEAF

$^1/_4$ CUP FRESH-SQUEEZED
    LEMON JUICE

$^1/_2$ TSP. SALT

$^1/_2$ TSP. FRESH-GROUND
    BLACK PEPPER

1 CUP VEGETABLE OIL

1 TSP. SESAME OIL

Salad

4 RIPE AVOCADOS,
    PEELED & SEEDED

2 HEADS BOSTON BIBB
    LETTUCE, CORED
    & RINSED

1 CUP CARROTS,
    $^1/_4$" JULIENNE

1 CUP JICAMA,
    $^1/_4$" JULIENNE

Directions:

Wheat Beer Dressing

1. IN A SAUCEPAN, BRING BEER TO A LOW SIMMER. ADD BAY LEAF AND REMOVE FROM HEAT. ALLOW TO STEEP FOR 20 MINUTES.

2. DISCARD BAY LEAF. POUR LIQUID INTO A BLENDER WITH LEMON JUICE, SALT AND PEPPER.

3. WITH BLENDER RUNNING AT MEDIUM SPEED, SLOWLY POUR OILS INTO BLENDER UNTIL EMULSIFIED.

Salad

1. CAREFULLY PRESS A SERRATED KNIFE INTO EACH AVOCADO UNTIL IT MAKES CONTACT WITH THE SEED. HOLDING THE KNIFE AGAINST THE SEED, ROTATE THE FRUIT TO SPLIT IT IN HALF LENGTHWISE.

2. SEPARATE THE TWO HALVES WITH A SLIGHT TWIST, WHICH WILL LEAVE THE WHOLE SEED IMBEDDED IN ONE OF THE HALVES. WITH A SPOON, CAREFULLY SCOOP OUT THE SEED, LEAVING THE FLESH INTACT.

3. HOLD EACH AVOCADO HALF SKIN-SIDE DOWN AND INSERT THE SPOON BETWEEN THE SKIN AND FLESH. RUN THE SPOON AROUND THE ENTIRE FRUIT, SEPARATING THE SKIN FROM THE FLESH. REPEAT WITH REMAINING AVOCADO HALVES.

4. PLACE EACH HALF, FLAT-SIDE DOWN, ON A CUTTING BOARD AND SLICE LENGTHWISE INTO $^1/_2$" SLICES.

5. ARRANGE LETTUCE LEAVES EQUALLY ON PLATES.

6. MIX TOGETHER CARROTS AND JICAMA. DIVIDE EQUALLY, MAKING NESTS IN THE CENTER OF LETTUCE LEAVES.

7. PLACE AVOCADO SLICES AROUND NESTS LIKE A TEPEE.

8. DRIZZLE DRESSING OVER THE SALAD AND SERVE.

> **Note:** *Selecting a ripe avocado is the most important step. It should be firm, not soft, with the squeeze resistance of a ripe peach or nectarine.*

CARNE ASADA

SERVES: 6

Directions:

1. WHISK MARINADE INGREDIENTS AND POUR OVER STEAKS IN A SHALLOW PAN.

2. MARINATE AT LEAST OVERNIGHT.

3. GRILL SIRLOINS TO DESIRED TEMPERATURE.

4. WHILE STEAKS ARE COOKING, HEAT THE OLIVE OIL AND SAUTÉ PEPPERS AND ONIONS IN A HOT SKILLET UNTIL SLIGHTLY BROWNED.

5. SEASON WITH SALT AND PEPPER TO TASTE.

6. TOP STEAKS WITH THE VEGETABLES AND SERVE WITH LIME WEDGES AND WARM FLOUR TORTILLAS.

Ingredients:

Marinade:
1/2 CUP OLIVE OIL

1/2 CUP LIME JUICE

1 TBSP. FRESH-GROUND BLACK PEPPER

1 TBSP. SALT

1 TBSP. GROUND CUMIN

2 TBSP. FRESH GARLIC, MINCED

6 (8-10 OZ.) TOP SIRLOIN STEAKS, ALL FAT TRIMMED

Topping:
2 TBSP. OLIVE OIL

2 LARGE RED BELL PEPPERS, JULIENNED

2 LARGE GREEN BELL PEPPERS, JULIENNED

1 JUMBO YELLOW ONION, JULIENNED

SALT & PEPPER TO TASTE

LIME WEDGES FOR GARNISH

12 FLOUR TORTILLAS

SERVES: 6

COCONUT RUM FLAN

Ingredients:

1 CUP WATER

1 CUP GRANULATED
 SUGAR

12 OZ. MILK

6 EGGS

1/4 CUP DARK RUM

1 CAN (14 OZ.)
 CONDENSED MILK

1 1/2 CUPS COCONUT
 MILK

1/2 CUP TOASTED
 COCONUT

Directions:

1. PREHEAT OVEN TO 325°.

1. PLACE WATER AND SUGAR IN A SAUCE PAN OVER HIGH HEAT.
 BRING TO A BOIL AND LET COOK, WITHOUT STIRRING, FOR
 10 MINUTES UNTIL LIGHT BROWN IN COLOR.

2. QUICKLY POUR CARAMEL INTO A 6 CUP FLAN RING OR 6
 RAMEKINS. LET COOL COMPLETELY.

3. DIVIDE TOASTED COCONUT INTO THE PREPARED MOLD(S)
 AND SET THEM INTO A PAN WITH 2" SIDES.

4. HEAT MILK OVER MEDIUM-HIGH HEAT. WHISK EGGS WITH
 RUM, CONDENSED MILK AND COCONUT MILK. SLOWLY WHISK
 HOT MILK INTO THE EGG MIXTURE A LITTLE AT A TIME TO
 AVOID SCRAMBLING THE EGGS.

5. POUR THE HOT EGG-MILK MIXTURE INTO THE PREPARED
 FLAN RING OR RAMEKINS. FILL EVENLY, USING ALL MIX.

6. PLACE THE FLAN RING OR RAMEKINS IN A BAIN MARIE
 ("WATER BATH": A 2" HIGH ROASTING PAN FILLED HALFWAY
 UP WITH HOT WATER).

7. BAKE AT 325° FOR ABOUT 45 MINUTES OR UNTIL SET, WITH
 THE CENTERS A LITTLE WIGGLY.

8. REMOVE FROM WATER BATH AND COOL TO ROOM
 TEMPERATURE.

9. COVER AND CHILL AT LEAST 4 HOURS OR OVERNIGHT.

10. WHEN READY TO SERVE, RUN A KNIFE BLADE AROUND THE
 EDGE OF THE FLAN AND PLACE A SERVING PLATE ON TOP
 OF THE PAN. QUICKLY INVERT. THE CARAMEL WILL RELEASE
 THE FLAN, CREATING A GOLDEN POOL OF TO BE ENJOYED.

11. SERVE WITH A LITTLE WHIPPED CREAM AND GARNISH WITH
 MORE TOASTED COCONUT IF DESIRED.

BLUE MOON MARGARITAS

YIELD: 1 PITCHER

Directions:

1. IN A PITCHER FILLED WITH ICE, ADD TEQUILA, ORANGE LIQUEUR, BLUE CURACAO AND SWEET AND SOUR.

2. STIR WELL AND POUR INTO SALT-RIMMED GLASSES.

3. SQUEEZE IN FRESH LIME WEDGE AND GARNISH WITH AN ORANGE WHEEL.

Fresh Sweet & Sour Mix

1 3/4 CUP SUGAR

1 1/2 QTS. WATER

1 TBSP. HONEY

1 1/2 CUPS FRESH-SQUEEZED LEMON JUICE

1 1/2 CUPS FRESH-SQUEEZED LIME JUICE

1. MIX TOGETHER AND KEEP REFRIGERATED.

Ingredients:

1 CUP GOLD TEQUILA
  (OR MORE TO TASTE)

3 OZ. ORANGE LIQUEUR

3 OZ. BLUE CURACAO

3 CUPS SWEET & SOUR MIX
  (MAKE FRESH OR
  USE BOTTLED)

Rosemary Skewered Sea Scallops
on Wild Greens

Chile Rubbed Steak
with Baja Shrimp Sauce

Espresso Crème Brulée

Romantic Dinner for Two

In this increasingly busy world, we all know how rare it is to find the time for a meal alone with someone special. Set the stage for the evening with a wonderful bottle of wine, lots of candles and a little mood music. And so you don't waste a moment, cook dinner together to make the most of the opportunity.

After a delicious appetizer of *Rosemary Skewered Sea Scallops on Wild Greens with Rosemary Vinaigrette,* serve the *Chile Rubbed Steak* with our favorite *Baja Shrimp Sauce. Espresso Crème Brulée* is the perfect end to the meal.

ROSEMARY SKEWERED SEA SCALLOPS ON WILD GREENS

Directions:

Skewers

1. TOSS SCALLOPS WITH OLIVE OIL, SALT AND PEPPER.

2. RENDER BACON BY COOKING SLIGHTLY OVER LOW HEAT. COOL, RESERVING FAT. IF USING PROSCIUTTO DO NOT RENDER.

3. WHEN BACON IS COOLED, WRAP AROUND EACH SCALLOP.

4. TO MAKE THE ROSEMARY SKEWERS, TRIM ALL BUT 2" OF LEAVES AT THE TOP OF EACH SPRIG, LEAVING THE LOWER END EXPOSED TO SKEWER THE SCALLOPS. CUT THE LOWER TIP OF THE STEM TO TO A SLANTED POINT.

5. AS SCALLOPS ARE WRAPPED, SKEWER 2 EACH ONTO THE ROSEMARY SKEWERS.

6. LET REST WHILE PREPARING GREENS AND VINAIGRETTE.

Greens

1. HEAT RESERVED BACON FAT OR BUTTER AND OIL IN SKILLET.

2. ADD SHALLOTS AND GARLIC. STIR UNTIL FRAGRANT.

3. TOSS IN CHARD OR SPINACH. SEASON WITH SALT AND PEPPER.

4. TOSS UNTIL WILTED AND COOK GENTLY FOR ABOUT 2-3 MINUTES THEN ADD MESCULEN GREENS.

5. GRILL SCALLOPS OVER HIGH HEAT OR BROIL UNTIL BACON IS CRISPY. ARRANGE GREENS ON TWO SALAD PLATES, TOP WITH SKEWERS AND DRIZZLE WITH ROSEMARY VINAIGRETTE (PAGE 116).

Ingredients:

Skewers

4 JUMBO SEA SCALLOPS (MORE IF NOT JUMBO)

1 TBSP. OLIVE OIL

1/4 TSP. SALT (OR TO TASTE)

1/4 TSP. FRESH-GROUND BLACK PEPPER (OR TO TASTE)

2 PIECES WILD BOAR BACON OR PROSCIUTTO, THINLY SLICED AND HALVED

2 (6") LONG ROSEMARY SPRIGS

Greens

RESERVED RENDERED FAT OR 1 TSP. EACH BUTTER AND OLIVE OIL

1 TBSP. SHALLOTS

1 CLOVE GARLIC, SMASHED & CHOPPED

1 CUP CHARD OR SPINACH, WASHED & SLICED 1/2" X 3" (LEAVES ONLY)

SALT & PEPPER TO TASTE

2 CUPS MESCULEN GREENS

SERVES: 2

Ingredients:

Rosemary Vinaigrette

1 SPRIG ROSEMARY

$1/3$ CUP CHICKEN OR
FISH STOCK

2 TBSP. RICE OR SHERRY
VINEGAR

1 TBSP. WHOLE-GRAIN
MUSTARD

1 TBSP. DIJON MUSTARD

6 TBSP. OLIVE OIL

SALT & PEPPER TO TASTE

Directions:

Rosemary Vinaigrette

1. PLACE ROSEMARY IN HOT SKILLET AND SAUTÉ QUICKLY, BEING CAREFUL NOT TO BURN.

2. ADD STOCK AND BRING TO A SIMMER. TURN OFF, COVER AND LET STEEP FOR 5 MINUTES. REMOVE SPRIG AND DISCARD.

3. WHISK VINEGAR AND MUSTARDS TOGETHER. SLOWLY WHISK IN ABOUT 2-3 TBSP. OF THE WARM STOCK TO THIS MIXTURE.

4. WHILE CONTINUING TO WHISK, BEGIN ADDING OIL UNTIL FULLY EMULSIFIED. SEASON WITH SALT AND PEPPER.

Note: If vinaigrette is too thick, more stock may be added until it reaches the desired consistency.

CHILE RUBBED STEAK WITH BAJA SHRIMP SAUCE

SERVES: 2

Directions:

Baja Shrimp Sauce (YIELD: 2-3 CUPS)

1. IN A LARGE SKILLET, HEAT OIL AND SAUTE CORN, POBLANOS, ONIONS AND GARLIC.
2. COOK OVER MEDIUM-HIGH HEAT FOR ABOUT 5 MINUTES UNTIL CRISP-TENDER.
3. DEGLAZE PAN BY ADDING THE SHERRY AND STIRRING TO LOOSEN ANY BROWNED BITS.
4. ADD CREAM, HERBS AND SPICES. BRING TO A BOIL. ADD TOMATOES.
5. REDUCE FOR 3-4 MINUTES, THEN STIR IN THE CORNSTARCH WHICH HAS BEEN DISSOLVED IN THE MILK.
6. COOK 2 MINUTES MORE UNTIL SAUCE THICKENS SLIGHTLY. (CAN BE PREPARED IN ADVANCE.)
7. WHEN READY TO SERVE, STIR IN ASPARAGUS TIPS AND COOKED SHRIMP AND HEAT THROUGH.
8. SERVE IMMEDIATELY, OVER STEAKS (BELOW). ALSO GREAT OVER YOUR FAVORITE CUT OF GRILLED FISH OR CHICKEN.

Steaks

2 (8-12 OZ.) TENDERLOIN OR NY STRIP STEAKS

2 TBSP. MUSTANG SPICE™*

1 CUP BAJA SHRIMP SAUCE

1. RUB STEAKS ALL OVER WITH MUSTANG SPICE™ AND LET SIT 20 MINUTES.
2. GRILL TO DESIRED TEMPERATURE AND TOP WITH HEATED BAJA SHRIMP SAUCE (ABOVE).

* See page 87 for Mustang Spice™ recipe.

Ingredients:

Baja Shrimp Sauce

1 TBSP. OLIVE OIL

1 LARGE EAR FRESH CORN, ROASTED & CUT FROM COB

1/2 CUP POBLANO PEPPERS, 1/4" DICE

1/2 CUP ONIONS, 1/2" DICE

1 CLOVE GARLIC, MINCED

2 TBSP. CREAM SHERRY OR DRY WHITE WINE

2 CUPS HEAVY CREAM

2 CUPS FRESH CILANTRO, CHOPPED (OPTIONAL)

1/2 TSP. OREGANO

2 TSP. MUSTANG SPICE™*

1/2 TSP. SALT (OR TO TASTE)

1/4 TSP. FRESH-GROUND BLACK PEPPER

1/2 CUP FRESH TOMATO, 1/2" DICE

1 TBSP. CORNSTARCH

2 TBSP. MILK

8 SPEARS ASPARAGUS, CUT ON 1/4" BIAS

1 CUP SHRIMP, DEVEINED, SHELLED & COOKED (OR CRAWFISH OR CRABMEAT)

ENJOYING WINE WITH SOUTHWEST FOOD

With its strong Spanish and Mexican influences, Southwest food is most often associated with beer and margaritas. While we serve and love both beverages with our cuisine, a well-selected bottle of wine can be like the wonderful sauce that completes the perfect Southwest dish.

Just like a sauce, wine can do three things: compete with, compliment, or contrast with a meal's flavors. If a wine competes with the food, neither wins, but when a wine compliments or contrasts with food, either effect can be very pleasing to the palate.

Southwest cuisine has many earthy flavors (dried chiles, chile rubs, roasted nuts, oven-roasting, grilling, etc.), subtle vegetable tones (corn, fresh chiles, squash) and heat elements (chiles). With this in mind, it is no wonder wine can be such a compliment to our recipes.

A peppery red wine can provide a complimentary flavor by increasing the subtle earthy spiciness of a rich mole sauce. This same dish may be contrasted with a light, crisp Fume Blanc or an even sweeter Riesling. In fact, sparkling wines go wonderfully with many spicy dishes adding the texture of the bubbles to play with the many flavors of the food.

While of today's popular varieties such as Chardonnay and Cabernet Sauvignon do not work as well with the food because of their heavy oak notes, Merlots, Sangioveses, Zinfandels (both red and medium-sweet whites), Rieslings, and Sparkling wines can each evoke different and wonderful characteristics of Southwest food. As with any culinary experience, experimentation is the key to discovering the right wine for your tastes.

Espresso Crème Brulée

Serves: 6

Directions:

1. Preheat oven to 325°.

2. Slit vanilla bean lengthwise.

3. Heat cream, sugar, espresso powder and vanilla bean until hot enough to dissolve sugar.

4. Meanwhile, beat egg yolks and vanilla extract until smooth.

5. Strain out vanilla bean from cream mixture.

6. Reserve bean and scrape out seeds. Add seeds back to cream mixture and stir to incorporate.

7. Temper the egg yolks by adding just a little of the hot cream mixture to equalize the temperature. This will keep the eggs from "scrambling" when the rest of the hot mixture is added. Then add the rest of the cream and mix well.

8. Pour into 6 small ramekins. Place them in a bain marie ("water bath": a 2" high roasting pan filled halfway up with hot water).

9. Bake at 325° for 20-30 minutes until firm, but still a little wiggly in the center.

10. Remove ramekins from water and chill for a minimum of 4 hours or overnight.

11. Sift sugar onto top. Using a torch or broiler, quickly brown to caramelize sugar.

12. Garnish with a few raspberries or sliced strawberries. Serve immediately.

Ingredients:

Custard
1/2 vanilla bean, split

3 cups heavy cream

2/3 cup sugar

3 tbsp. instant espresso powder

8 large egg yolks

1 tbsp. vanilla extract

Topping
1/2 cup sugar

fresh raspberries or strawberries for garnish

Contributing Chefs

We wish to thank our chefs from around the country for
their creativity and ingenuity and for taking time from
their busy schedules to make this cookbook possible:

Jose Balduz	Alpharetta, Georgia
Jack Beeson	Kansas City, Missouri
Alex Colaianni	Corporate Chef
Doug Czufin	VP Culinary Department
Julio Diaz	Atlanta, Georgia
Tudie Frank-Johnson	Corporate Chef
Adrian Heuer	Denver, Colorado
Mickey Jamarillo	Friend of Sam's Cafe from New Mexico
Mike Lane, General Manager	Denver, Colorado
Damon LeMaster	Seattle, Washington
Jaime Lopez	Nashville, Tennessee
David Lunsford	St. Louis, Missouri
Kevin MacLaren	Glendale, California
Mario Maldonado	Dallas, Texas
Jeff Mc Burney	Redmond, Washington
Irving Oliver	Arizona Center, Phoenix, Arizona
Debbie Ponce	Austin, Texas
Leonel Reyes	Houston, Texas
James Venezia	San Antonio, Texas
Brian Wright	Broomfield, Colorado
Larry Yonda	Biltmore, Phoenix, Arizona

ACHIOTE PASTE
Seeds of the Annatto Tree from Central America that have been ground into a moist paste which is usually sold in bricks. Adds a distinct but non-spicy flavor to classic dishes. It is what gives cheddar cheese its trademark color and is also used to color butter.

ANCHO CHILES
Dried *poblano peppers* that have been left on the plant to ripen until red and then sun dried to a very dark, almost black, color—the main ingredient of Mole Poblano. *(See Poblano Pepper)*

ASADERO CHEESE
A fresh Mexican cheese, slightly aged and tangy in flavor. It is very good melted, used for dips, enchiladas, quesadillas and for stuffing empanadas or chile rellenos. If you can't find Asadero, Monterey Jack cheese may be substituted.

CALABASITAS
A traditional squash dish, usually made of a green Mexican squash stewed with green pepper, onion, jalapeños, corn and tomatoes. Our version is a new interpretation of an old favorite.

CANELA STICKS
Mexican cinnamon, "Canela" can be found in ethnic or gourmet sections of grocery stores and smells like Red Hot candies. If unavailable, regular cinnamon can be substituted.

CHIPOTLE CHILES
Jalapeños that have been ripened to red and then dried and smoked over fire. The chiles are sold dry or rehydrated and canned in a rich tomato-vinegar sauce called "Adobo."

CHORIZO
Mexican chorizo is a sausage typically made of pork, chile, paprika and salt. Many brands are available, raw or smoked, made with pork, beef, or turkey. If using uncooked, cook and drain off the oil before using in egg dishes. Chorizos can vary in heat from mild to wild. They can be found in natural casings or in plastic sleeves.

COTIJA CHEESE
A firm, crumbly white Mexican cheese with a flavor similar to Greek Feta but drier and not as salty. Use to crumble on tacos, enchiladas, refried beans and salads. If Cotija is unavailable, Feta cheese can be substituted.

EMPANADAS
Crisp pastries in the shape of half-moons. They can be savory or sweet, small or large. They be stuffed with a variety of fillings and then baked or fried. Similar to a turn-over.

GUAJILLO CHILES
Usually only found dry. Guajillo chiles have a citrusy flavor and are well suited for seafood. They are medium hot in spice with shiny, thin red walls, usually 5"- 6" in length.

HABANERO CHILES
The smaller they are, the hotter they get! A bright flavored, tropical chile weed found throughout the Yucatan. Very distinct flavor—one of the hottest chiles cultivated today. Use in fruit-based sauces, salsas and marinades. Beware—extremely hot. Use when the 1" chile ripens to an orange-red.

JALAPEÑOS
The "work horse" of green chiles. Medium to hot in spice. Waxy, dark green, with a fresh flavor that is distinctly jalapeño. Remove seeds and veins to reduce some of the heat.

JICAMA
This bulbous vegetable is often called the "Mexican potato." It has thin, brown skin and crisp, white flesh. Raw or cooked, it has a sweet, nutty flavor. When raw, it should be peeled immediately before serving. It makes a delicious appetizer when dipped in fresh lime juice and chile-powder. Cooked, jicama has a texture similar to a water chestnut.

MASA & MASA HARINA
Fresh prepared Masa is corn that has been soaked in slabbed lime water and then ground to form a moist thick dough. Masa Harina is a corn meal made from dehydrated Masa that has been ground very fine. If fresh Masa is unavailable use Masa Harina mixed 50/50 with water and proceed as above.

MEXICAN CHOCOLATE
A hard, sugary chocolate made with *Canela*. It is usually sold in large-size tablets that can be dissolved in hot milk or grated into cake batters or onto bakery items. If unavailable, bittersweet chocolate and cinnamon can be substituted.

MOLE
A complex sauce based on chiles, onions, nuts, corn, fruit and usually chocolate that is spiced with aromatics. The sauce is pureed smooth and simmered and stirred for a long time to develop the rich, earthy flavors. It is widely served as a celebration dish all over Mexico. There are many types of Mole, with Mole Poblano from Oaxaca being the most popular.

MUSTANG SPICE™
Mustang Spice™ is available from your favorite Canyon Cafe, Sam's Cafe, or Desert Fire Restaurants. You may make your own by using 1/2 cup each of New Mexican Red Chile Powder and Cajun Blackening Spice and 1 Tbsp. salt.

New Mexican Red Chiles
Long, ripe red Anaheim-type chiles, grown mainly around Hatch, New Mexico where they develop their medium heat. Sun dried and sold in whole pods or ground form—known as "New Mexican Red Chile Powder."

Nopalitos
Young, tender Prickly Pear cactus pads—be careful of the thorns! The canned variety is already sliced with the thorns removed. Napolitos taste somewhat like green beans and are frequently used in salads and in pork dishes with chiles.

Panko Crumbs
Coarse, white, crispy, air-dried, bread crumbs. You can substitute unseasoned, coarse bread crumbs.

Poblano Peppers
Fresh, large, dark green chile peppers with rounded shoulder tapering to tip. Medium to spicy hot. Great peeled, seeded and stuffed for chili rellenos. When dry they are called *Ancho Chilies*, a must for making *Moles*.

Prickly Pears
A flat leafed cacti that produces beautiful flowers and very sweet fruit that is usually used to flavor drinks, vinaigrettes, jellies and candies. The fresh fruits are available seasonally and are best prepared by peeling off the skin and thorns, chopping or pureeing the flesh, and then straining to remove the seeds. Bottled juice/syrup can be found year-round at specialty stores. The young pads are known as *Nopalitos* and taste somewhat like green beans.

Queso Fresco
A fresh, unaged cows' milk from Mexico with a mild, creamy flavor. It is usually packed in whey and crumbles well.

Serrano Chiles
Slender, light-green chile peppers, usually 1 1/2" to 3" long. Can pack a punch! Considered to be medium-hot. Use seeds and all—sparingly. Has a very clean fresh taste.

Sopes
Fat little Masa boats with pinched-up edges, similar to a pie shell, but not very deep.

Tomatillos
This small green fruit is a member of the nightshade family and looks much like its cousin, the tomato, except that it has a thin, parchment-like husk. Also called the "Mexican Green Tomato," the tomatillo can be used cooked or raw to enhance salsas, guacamoles and other sauces. Although they will ripen to deep yellow, tomatillos are usually used while still green and firm.